First-Time Filmmaker F*#^-Ups

Navigating the Pitfalls to Making a Great Movie

Daryl Bob Goldberg

ELSEVIER

AMSTERDAM • BOSTON • HEIDELBERG • LONDON
NEW YORK • OXFORD • PARIS • SAN DIEGO
SAN FRANCISCO • SINGAPORE • SYDNEY • TOKYO

Focal Press is an imprint of Elsevier

Focal
Press

Focal Press is an imprint of Elsevier
225 Wyman Street, Waltham, MA 02451
The Boulevard, Langford Lane, Kidlington, Oxford, OX5 1GB, UK

Notices
Knowledge and best practice in this field are constantly changing. As new research and experience broaden our understanding, changes in research methods, professional practices, or medical treatment may become necessary.

Practitioners and researchers must always rely on their own experience and knowledge in evaluating and using any information, methods, compounds, or experiments described herein. In using such information or methods they should be mindful of their own safety and the safety of others, including parties for whom they have a professional responsibility.

To the fullest extent of the law, neither the Publisher nor the authors, contributors, or editors, assume any liability for any injury and/or damage to persons or property as a matter of products liability, negligence or otherwise, or from any use or operation of any methods, products, instructions, or ideas contained in the material herein.

Library of Congress Cataloging-in-Publication Data
Application submitted.

British Library Cataloguing-in-Publication Data
A catalogue record for this book is available from the British Library.

ISBN: 978-0-240-81923-5

For information on all Focal Press publications
visit our website at *www.elsevierdirect.com*

Typeset by: diacriTech, Chennai, India

Printed in the United States of America
11 12 13 14   5 4 3 2 1

First-Time Filmmaker F*#^-Ups

Dedication

This book is dedicated to my family and friends, who support me through all my *Fuck-Ups*.

Inna, Dad, Mom, Louis, Karie, and Uncle Buggy.

Eric Berkal, Peter Tulba, Tim Hood, Dan Taggatz, Dennis McGonagle, and Lauren Mattos.

Contents

Contents

PART 4 SCHEDULING

PART 5 BUDGETING

PART 6 ACTING

Contents

Contents

Preface

Countless people fantasize about making movies. However, only a tiny percent of them will ever sincerely attempt to make one. This book is for those few who would like to do more than just dream or talk about making movies. It's for those who want to live that dream—without fucking it all up along the way, as is far too often the case.

This book is the road map that will enable you to avoid the potholes and detours that prevent filmmaker after filmmaker from making their movie—or accomplishing the task as successfully as they could have. It's the resource I wish had existed when I made my first feature film.

I encourage you to read this book in its entirety. Even if you are interested only in how to get your movie started, not planning for the entire process is just one of the many common fuck-ups you're about to learn how to avoid.

After you've read the book, periodically revisit the sections that correspond to the stage of the process you're approaching. You may be surprised just how frequently your movie is presenting you with the very problems contained in these pages. Problems, that by reading this book, you can avoid falling victim to.

Anyone who has ever done it will tell you that making a movie is a long and difficult road to travel. However, I promise you that the journey can be every bit as rewarding as the destination.

Getting Started

Fuck-Up #1

"I Can't Make a Movie"
Why you (yes, you) can make a movie

"Wisdom begins in wonder."[1]
—Socrates

The Fuck-Up…

Like most things in life, your ability to make a movie lies not in what you know but in what you are willing to learn. If you have a willingness to learn and the ambition to see it through, then have no doubt, if you truly want to make a movie badly enough, you can.

Don't believe me yet? That's okay. Throughout this book, we'll discuss the pitfalls that prevent aspiring filmmakers from accomplishing their dreams. More importantly, we'll learn how to avoid them.

How to Do It Right…

Let's dispel two of the biggest reasons people think they can't make movies right away:

1. Lack of connections
2. Lack of experience

Connections and experience are helpful—and not just when it comes to making movies. Nevertheless, neither of these excuses should prevent your filmmaking dreams. Here's why…

Connections

The list of successful Hollywood bigwigs who grew up already deeply connected within Tinseltown is long. But guess what? There is an even longer list of Hollywood players who got into the industry with no connections whatsoever. The truth is there is no mythical wall trying to keep you out of the world of filmmaking. In fact, the film industry is known for its passionate love of the new: the industry is always hunting for the next hot new actor/writer/director/shoe/car/club/drug. If you have talent, ambition, and (most important of all) can make them a buck—then the industry will want to find you. You just have to make sure they can. And that, for an aspiring filmmaker, starts with making your movie.

James Cameron was a truck driver, Quentin Tarantino famously was a video store clerk, and even the late-great Orson Welles had no actual connections when he took it upon himself to stride into a theater in Dublin and simply proclaim he was a Broadway star in order to start his career out of absolutely nothing. It wasn't who they knew that got them started. It was a lot of ambition, a little bit of luck, and the talent to back it all up. They certainly didn't use their lack of connections as an excuse not to try, so neither should you.

Experience

Stanley Kubrick once said, "One of the things that gave me the most confidence in trying to make a film was seeing all the lousy films that I saw. Because I sat there and thought, 'Well, I don't know a goddamn thing about movies, but I know I can make a film better than that.'"[2] Woody Allen wrote, "I have no idea what I am doing. But incompetence has never prevented me from plunging in with enthusiasm."[3] The truth is that everyone must start somewhere, even if that somewhere is nowhere.

Mr. Kubrick's advice on the matter was simple, "Perhaps it sounds ridiculous, but the best thing that young filmmakers should do is to get hold of a camera and…make a movie of any kind at all."[4] James Cameron put it similarly. "Shoot something. No matter how small, no matter how cheesy, no matter whether your friends and your sister star in it. Shoot it on video if you have to. Put your name on it as director. Now you're a director."[5] The story remains the same nearly every time; the only way to truly make yourself a "director" is by directing, and the only way to make yourself a "producer" is by producing.

Furthermore, inexperience comes with its own huge advantages. When I was filming my first movie, I had raised about $250,000. Had I known then what I know now, I would have realized the movie I was filming should cost a lot more than that and I would have given up before I started. I was too naïve to know I shouldn't be able to do it, so I went ahead and did it anyway. Movie accomplished. The same goes for a lot of filmmaking: if we don't know it's supposed to be impossible, then we won't be discouraged from trying and achieving it. Experienced people will not hesitate to tell you what you can and cannot do—not believing them can be a powerful force.

Inexperience is truly a problem only if we fail to recognize what it is we do not know. Socrates taught, "True wisdom comes to each of us when we realize how little we understand."[6] You are already on your way by getting proactive, picking up this book, and having a willingness to learn. You're taking a tremendous step on the path to making your movie. Now keep walking.

Key Points

- If you want to make a movie badly enough, you can.
- Most successful people in the industry made it with no prior connections.
- Inexperience can be a resource.
- If you don't know something is supposed to be impossible, you're likely to try and possibly achieve it.
- Experience is not crucial, but a willingness to learn is.

Fuck-Up #2

"I *Just* Want to Make a Movie"

How to pick the right project for you and your career

"If you want to make God laugh, tell him about your plans."[7]
—Woody Allen

The Fuck-Up...

Countless new filmmakers set out to make a movie—devoting vast amounts of time, effort, and their soul to the process—only to realize, somewhere along the way, that they picked the wrong project to pursue.

Before embarking on your own long and arduous filmmaking journey, take some time to evaluate the project you're about to put so much into. Can you pull it off? Will it showcase your talent and make good use of your resources? Will it be able to find an audience? And will it help your career?

How to Do It Right...

When a screenwriter friend and I embarked on our first movie, we picked a large-scale kid's adventure film. We had a script, a business plan, and a lot of enthusiasm. But as we started fund-raising, we realized we wouldn't be able to put together anywhere near the amount of money this film needed. So we went back to the drawing board and asked ourselves, "What can we make for the money we think we can really raise?" We ended up successfully making and distributing a low-budget thriller called *Unholy* starring scream queen Adrienne Barbeau (*The Fog, Escape from New York, Creepshow*).

I had fallen victim to a classic new filmmaker mistake: setting out to make a movie I could never pull off. However, I adapted my plan to my circumstances, so everything worked out fine. And you should take a moment to consider doing the same. A lot of new filmmakers are obsessed with a particular project or idea and insist upon pursuing a movie they can't actually pull off. It's critical that you set out to make a movie you actually can make. This advice may sound obvious, but you'd be shocked how often new filmmakers fail to take this into consideration.

Throughout this book we'll discuss topics such as how you can go about raising money and other keys to making your film. As we discuss these ideas, try to determine your and your team's ability to accomplish these tasks and how it applies to your movie. What fundraising ideas are you willing to consider? What level of production, time, and effort are you willing to undertake? Make sure your project fits those limitations, and if it doesn't, consider adapting it—or changing projects entirely.

If you think you can put together $1,000, then setting out to make a $1,000 movie is a good idea. And if you think you can raise $100 million, then set out to make a $100 million movie. By all means, be ambitious, daring, and innovative. After all, that is what is most likely to get a new filmmaker noticed. But also embrace your limitations, not for the manner in which they'll limit you, but for the way they'll challenge you to come up with something great that you can really pull off.

Next, think about how the project you've chosen will help you and your career. Far too many new filmmakers can focus only on how desperately they want to get a movie made. However, chances are, you don't want to make just one movie; you'd like to eventually make a second and third, and so on. So consider carefully what is likely to showcase your talent and get your career rolling. What will make people take notice of you, and what you are capable of? What will show your particular creativity, talent, and ability? What's likely to inspire someone to give you your next film? Don't focus on making just the one movie; think of your first film as a career path and decide what you'd like that path to look like.

Chances are, you're not doing all this hard work because you intend for only your friends and family to see the finished product. If you want your film to be a career move, it has to be something that other people will actually want to watch. That is not to say you should solely aim to make a copycat of other successful movies. I'm a firm believer that if you make the film you think other people will want to see, you're likely to fail; you can never please everyone. However, if you set out to make a movie that you want to see, you have an excellent chance at success. Therefore, the question to ask yourself is, "What is a movie that I want to see, that other people also want to see?"

You want your movie to showcase you, your vision, and your talent. Filmmakers are a brand: a "Tarantino movie," a "Hitchcock movie"—each has certain connotations. Although it can be very frustrating to be forced into a category, it's no less a reality of how the industry works. This is especially true when talking about your first movie. More established directors and producers might get the opportunity to make movies of different genres to show the range of what they are capable of. But if you are making your first film, think carefully about what you'd like that first impression to be.

Finally, when picking a project, you need to consider the reality of what it'll take to bring your ideas to the screen. Which leads us to our next *Fuck-Up*...

Key Points

- A movie is a lot of work, so pick a project worthy of your time and effort.
- Set out to accomplish an ambitious project—as well as one that you can actually pull off.
- Think about how the project will help your career.
- Set out to make a movie that shows your talent.
- Set out to make a movie that people will want to see.
- Think about what it'll take to bring the page to the screen.

Fuck-Up #3

"The Script Is Done"
Why the script is never really 'done'

"Sit down, and put down everything that comes into your head and then you're a writer. But an author is one who can judge his own stuff's worth, without pity, and destroy most of it."[8]

—Colette

The Fuck-Up...

You may already have a good idea about what movie you would like to make. You may even already have a script. But where many new filmmakers go wrong is naively thinking that what's in their head or on the page will not, and/or should not, change.

Many inexperienced filmmakers believe that what they have imagined and written can and should translate completely unmolested into what they shoot, edit, and release. However, this notion has never actually been a reality throughout the entire history of filmmaking. Far too many variables affect the filmmaking process for ideas not to change during that process. Simply put, if you think you know how your movie is going to come out, you're wrong. You have a far better chance at accurately predicting the lottery for the next 100 years than how your movie will turn out.

Like it or not, your film will not be the exception to this rule. However, if you get yourself in a mindset that allows you and your movie to evolve and adapt to the many circumstances it will encounter, you will be in a position to make something far better than the movie you currently imagine.

How to Do It Right...

Throughout this book you will notice a recurring theme: the necessity for your ideas to adapt in order to survive. All films face problems, and if your movie can't evolve to take advantage of its circumstances, it will fall apart.

This spirit of evolution starts in the concept and screenplay stages and exists in every single stage that follows. The legendary Roger Corman, who has produced and directed hundreds of movies, once said, "I've never made the film I wanted to make. No matter what happens, it never turns out exactly as I hoped."[9]

New filmmakers often struggle with the realization that their vision must be adaptable. Yes, it is going to change, and it is going to hurt to watch your ideas become something other than what you expected, but it is all for the best. This may sound very dramatic, but anyone who has been through the experience can tell you that it can be painful to lose things that you love in your movie. However, a change that makes the scene or movie better is a necessary change. And changes that make the scene or movie accomplishable are absolute necessities. Adaptation is necessary to the process, and this starts in the script.

It costs the same amount of money to write "The audience sees a black screen and hears nothing" as it costs to write "300,000 giant alien monsters dance the Macarena in Yankee Stadium." But remember, you're not writing a novel; you intend to bring what is on the page to the screen.

(Forget the cost of making giant dancing alien monsters or renting Yankee Stadium as a location; clearing the music rights for the Macarena song alone could break the bank.) To make sure what you write can be put on the screen affordably, you must think about the realities of how you'll get the page to the screen.

Think creatively, and those limitations can inspire greatness. Gene Roddenberry wanted the crew to fly between the ship and the various planets they would be visiting when he created his TV show *Star Trek*, but when that idea proved too costly to shoot, he changed the script—and the iconic idea of "transporting" was born. Our restrictions often force us to think more creatively and spawn greater ideas. Like the Roman poet Horace wrote, "Adversity reveals genius, prosperity conceals it."[10] This is a phenomenon you will likely see recurring throughout your own filmmaking process. Embrace your limitations as opportunities to be creative, and doing so will certainly serve to benefit you and your project.

Something may look simple on paper and on the screen, but this does not mean that the steps between page and screen are by any means simple. If there is a way to write a scene that will make shooting it faster, you are already a step ahead. John Carpenter had the plane crash in *Escape from New York* shown on a computer monitor with wireframe images instead of attempting to visualize an actual plane crash. *Wet Hot American Summer* has an entire rescue scene hilariously played on a shot of bystanders reacting to a daring rescue, but never actually showing the rescue they are supposed to be witnessing. Or, for countless more examples of how to communicate much of your narrative without actually putting all of your action or dialogue on-screen, rent any number of Woody Allen films.

THE LINGO

Narrative: A story, whether true or fictitious.

Example: Some movies focus on the narrative; other films care less about story.

You can also save time and money with what you do choose to show on-screen. If you've hung out on a few sets, you have likely already realized that performance and dialogue-driven scenes are generally faster to shoot than action scenes. Or that having to shoot a few actors versus many makes things go much faster. And having fewer locations saves a great deal of time and money; not just the cost of securing the spaces, but the hours and days traveling between and setting up multiple locations can quickly eat a large portion of one's schedule. Explosions, big set pieces, effects, hard-to-acquire locations, and stunts are all examples of elements that are likely to be cost prohibitive and thus may need to be evolved into other ideas within your screenplay.

Conversely, you can exploit the resources you do have. This is a great way of making your movie look as though it cost a lot more than it did. If you have a great location you can use for little or no money, write it into your script. If you are a special effects wizard and can do much of that labor yourself, put that in your script. If your grandmother owns a tank, great, use it. Tailor your script to your resources and write with that in mind. Push the envelope and make the most ambitious film possible, but remember the quality of the film is ultimately more important than its ambition. And being able to accomplish your plan is most important of all.

Often the best approach is to write with creative abandon, but to revise with your limitations in mind. New writers frequently get caught up in the pure joy of creation and forget the realities of what it will take to create what they are putting on the page. However, life will always be there to deliver a dose of reality and force you to adapt your ideas, like a young Steven Spielberg did when making the original blockbuster *Jaws*. Spielberg said:

> The difference between making Jaws 31 years ago and War of the Worlds is that today, anything I can imagine, I can realize on film. Then, when my mechanical shark was being repaired and I had to shoot something, I had to make the water scary. I relied on the audience's imagination, aided by where I put the camera. Today, it would be a digital shark. It would cost a hell of a lot more, but never break down. As a result, I probably would have used it four times as much, which would have made the film four times less scary. Jaws is scary because of what you don't see, not because of what you do.[11]

Key Points

- Your script must adapt to its circumstances to survive.
- Ideas, movies, and filmmakers all must also evolve to survive.
- Having your ideas change can be painful but necessary.
- Think about the realities of bringing the page to the screen.
- Saving time saves money.
- Find creative ways *not* to show expensive things on-screen.
- Exploit the resources you have.
- Limitation inspires creativity.
- Quality is more important than ambition.
- Write with creative abandon and revise with a more practical approach.

Fuck-Up #4

"I Can Do This Alone"

Why every movie is a collaborative process

"No man is an island."[12]

—John Donne

The Fuck-Up...

Making a movie is at least 100,000 times harder than most people expect. I've seen normal, intelligent, and hardworking people go absolutely out of their minds trying to make a movie. The truth is, it's hard, really hard. It can thoroughly drain your energy, time, emotions, and in some cases, wallet. And that's when you have help. I'd describe what it's like to do it alone, but nobody has ever actually accomplished that to tell the tale.

How to Do It Right...

Many aspiring filmmakers think that nobody is going to care about their movie like they do, that no one else will have the passion, commitment, energy, or time, and thus they are stuck going at it largely alone. Although it is absolutely true that you must be a motivating force behind every single step of the process, you do not need to be a solitary force. There are many people out there who would love to be part of making a movie and would even love to be a part of making your movie. Some of them do it for a living, some of them do it out of passion, and the truly lucky ones do it for both reasons. You must find the right people to help you on your moviemaking journey.

Because filmmaking is so difficult, passion is a key job requirement. Two different friends of mine wrote the first two films I produced and directed. They gave me not just great scripts, but great collaboration and motivation. Our collective passion was the force behind making those movies happen. Together we shared in the joys of each and every success, and the agony of every defeat. Involving someone who is passionate, and better yet has a vested interest in seeing the movie succeed, provides not just another person working to make the movie happen, but also emotional support. Making movies is a ride unlike anything else, and like all deeply emotional experiences, it's wonderful to be able to share them with people who will be equally affected.

Filmmaking is absolutely a collaborative art. Whether it is you and a few friends or a cast and crew of thousands, you are never going to make a movie alone. Even Robert Rodriguez, who wrote the wonderful and inspiring book *Rebel Without a Crew* about the making of his first film *El Mariachi,* in fact had a crew, albeit an amateur one of very supportive friends and family.

It greatly aids filmmakers to realize that they must not operate in solitude. Embrace that the cast, crew, and others are there to help, and often that help comes in a creative form. You involve people with passion and expertise for a reason, and those are wonderful assets to utilize. Assure them that it is not just the director's or producer's work being made, but their work as well that will ultimately end up on the screen. Even the most controlling "auteurs" never truly work alone.

> **THE LINGO**
>
> **Auteur theory:** A French theory that a director should be the sole creator of a film in the same manner an author is the sole creator of a book.
>
> Example: The auteur theory ignores the fact that a film would be drastically different if the actors, locations, crew, or just about anything else were to change.

Not every person who's involved in your movie may be quite as passionate as you are about the project. There's a good chance some people will show up because working on a movie is a job and they need the money, because they're bored, or because you're offering free pizza. Although it's important to collaborate with as many passionate people as possible, what's most important is that the people who will be the day-to-day support and motivation behind your movie have passion. Don't let the bad apples spoil your movie-pie and remember there's a reason you've never seen anyone win an Oscar and not want to hug, kiss, or high-five someone else who was involved. It's not only misery that loves company.

Key Points

- You cannot make a movie alone.
- You will need others to help you with the workload and the emotional support.
- Involve at least one other person who also has a passionate and vested interest in the project's success.
- Don't be discouraged by those who do not share your passion.
- Embrace those who are there to help.

Fuck-Up #5

"My Buddy/Mom/Brother/Dog Is Going to Produce"
Why you desperately need a good producer and what that means

> "Experience is a hard teacher because she gives the test first, the lesson afterwards."[13]
> —Vernon Sander's Law

The Fuck-Up...

"Producer" is one of the most vaguely defined titles ever created. Because it sounds good and its meaning is ambiguous, a whole lot of people want to be called "producers" while simultaneously having no idea what the job actually entails.

Despite the difficulty in defining the term, one thing is certain, your film is nearly guaranteed to fall apart if the real producing responsibilities are given to the wrong person.

How to Do It Right...

There are many types of "producers." There are executive producers, assistant producers, associate producers, supervising producers, coordinating producers, line producers, co-producers, and co-executive assistant supervising coordinating line producers. Okay, I made up that last one, but you get the point: there are many kinds of producers, and it can be hard to know what any of these people actually do. And those simply called "producer" are the most mysterious of them all.

Look at the credits of any movie, and you are likely to see several people listed as producer. Chances are, out of these 3, 5, or 30 "producers," only a few did what you think of as hands-on producing. To "produce" something is to create it—the same way a carpenter produces a table or a mother produces a baby. But it is not necessarily creation in the creative sense. Remember, the carpenter who built the table may or may not be the person who designed it. Nature may have designed the baby, but the mother created it; she makes it possible. The same goes for the movies; making a movie happen is a real "producer's" job.

THE LINGO

IMDB: The Internet Movie Database available at *www.imdb.com* (if you've never explored it, I highly recommend you do so right away).

Example: IMDB is the résumé for most filmmakers.

Despite what the title should mean, the "producer" label is frequently given out for a myriad of reasons other than helping to "create" the movie in the hands-on creation sense of the word. Sometimes you'll give out different producing credits to encourage investment of varying degrees. A star might get a producing credit simply because she demands it. A director might even insist on giving a producing title to a boyfriend or girlfriend. Very often an actor's manager will want a producer credit (fortunately, agents are not allowed such credits, but managers can pretty much ask for anything because they are not regulated by a guild). These are just some of the many political reasons someone may garner the title "producer."

If you have to give out political producing credits, don't be surprised; most movies do. What is crucial is that you have on board at least one person who is really going to produce in the "creation" sense of the word—someone who is absolutely making sure your movie happens at every step.

Initially, making sure the movie happens largely has to do with packaging the key creative elements of a film, also known as the "above-the-line" elements. They include the film's screenplay, director, stars, and financing. It is in this sense that the producer is assembling the parts to enable the movie to be created.

> ## THE LINGO
>
> **Above-the-line:** The items in the budget that are considered critical to the project being greenlit. They often include the script, executive producer, producers, director, and stars of the film.
>
> **Below-the-line:** Every cost that is not above-the-line.
>
> Example: Below-the-line personnel are often considered replaceable. However, losing any above-the-line personnel may potentially cause the project to fall apart.

In the studio world, a producer's main work may stop after assembling those key parts and the moviemaking process is underway. Then the producer can hire people to do most of the day-to-day supervision. In the independent film world, a producer is often the one overseeing the details of a project long after the initial package and financing are put together. The producer guides the project through production, post-production, and distribution.

The problem comes when this key responsibility of being the film's *true* producer falls to someone who is ultimately incapable of this difficult job. Many inexperienced filmmakers give the real producing responsibilities to a friend, family member, boyfriend, girlfriend, or associate only to find that despite their personal closeness, that person simply isn't the right fit for the job.

So the question becomes, who is the right person? To greatly oversimplify the many facets of what it takes to be a truly effective producer, I suggest looking for three key traits:

1. **Passion:** Making a film is simply too damn hard for it to be successful without an unbelievable amount of passion. The obstacles are countless, and if the hands-on producer isn't

committed to seeing a movie through every step come hell or high water, the movie is going to have a difficult time surviving. This is a blood, sweat, and tears kind of commitment. So make sure your producer is as committed as possible because that commitment will be tested time and again.

2. **Ability:** Passion is wonderful, but if the person doesn't have the ability to make the things he or she is fighting for happen, that person is embarking on an impossible mission. A producer must be a born problem solver, someone who will look at any obstacle and never see defeat. This person must always be able to find a way to overcome any hurdle.

3. **Experience:** This whole book is an explanation of why inexperience causes newcomers to fuck up a lot. So let me put it simply, get someone experienced, and you can expect a lot fewer *Fuck-Ups*.

Key Points

- "Producer" is a very vague term.
- You need at least one person on your team who is going to be a "producer" in more than just title.
- "Producing" is creating. The producer must make sure the movie happens, no matter what.
- An incapable producer can destroy your movie.
- Don't give the producing responsibility to just anyone who is willing. Choose carefully.
- A good producer must have incredible amounts of passion and ability; experience helps, too.

Getting the Money

Fuck-Up #6

"I'll Never Get the Money"

How you can get the money to make your movie

"To hell with circumstances; I create opportunities."[1]

—Bruce Lee

The Fuck-Up...

Many would-be filmmakers end up never raising the money they need for their movie. Some don't even give it a try, thereby assuring their failure. Others sit back waiting for Hollywood to come knocking. I promise you, regardless of your talent or ability, if you're waiting for success to beat down your door, it is likely to be a very long wait.

You have to go out and get noticed. You really can raise money and make your movie, but you have to take the initiative and be the one knocking on doors. That task will likely require you to get more proactive than you have ever been.

How to Do It Right...

"How did you get the money?" is the most frequent question aspiring filmmakers pose to accomplished filmmakers. Most of the time, they are hoping for a simple answer that will tip them off to the magical pot of film financing gold beneath a rainbow that, until this point, nobody has bothered to mention to them. Unfortunately, that pot of gold just does not exist. There is no list of wealthy people who are dying to give you loads of cash to make your movie. Sure, it may be disappointing to hear, but there will be many more disappointments along the road to success—so better to get used to it now. Like the Japanese proverb says, "Fall down seven times and stand up eight."

Shortly, we'll discuss some good approaches to finding financing, all of which are helpful and none of which are easy answers or guarantees. Knowing that, if you are still willing to put forth the effort, you're off to a great start.

There is no road map to financing an independent film. We'll discuss some great ideas, but you should know from the outset that the only *simple* answer to "how to get the money" is "any way possible." Of course, "any way possible" is magically vague—and perhaps I should amend that to be "any way possible that you feel comfortable with"—because some means are more morally questionable than others. You have probably heard some of the popular stories about first-time filmmakers maxing out their credit cards, performing magnificent acts of insurance fraud and other criminal acts that make those things look like mere child's play. Kevin Smith's film *Clerks* was financed largely by credit card debt. Robert Rodriguez raised the money for *El Mariachi* by subjecting himself to paid medical experiments. *Deep Throat* was funded by the mob. And I am sure countless other movies, some successful and many more not, have been financed by means to which no one in his right mind will ever confess. There simply are no wrong ways to raise the money and that's because there's also no one way to do it. Independent film financing is not a well-defined step-by-step process, and although there are strategies for raising funds, "any way possible (that you feel morally comfortable with)" is also an acceptable answer. However, if knocking over a bank is not quite your style, other potential means of financing your movie do exist.

Family members are perhaps the most common investors for first-time filmmakers. Be forewarned, though: sitting across the Thanksgiving table from your grandmother whose life savings you lost can strain even the most loving family relationships. So make sure that, as with any investment, your family members can afford to lose 100 percent of their contribution. If they love you enough to take that risk and can afford to do so, that is truly wonderful and you should count yourself lucky. If you and they are okay with knowing they could lose every cent, by all means take the money gratefully and don't forget to call on their birthdays and holidays.

THE LINGO

Pitch: A brief presentation given to try to persuade someone to be involved in your project financially or otherwise.

Example: A filmmaker may start pitching a wacky comedy and end up pitching a period drama.

If you do not have any wealthy relatives, and that long lost uncle kicking off and leaving you a fat inheritance seems unlikely, it's time to look outside the family circle. You can improve the difficult odds of finding an investor by increasing your "proximity to power." Let's say you are a hairdresser but also an aspiring director. Cutting hair on a movie set is more likely to help you network than cutting hair in Nebraska. This may seem like a ludicrous example, if only it were not true: Mel Gibson actually let his hairdresser direct *Paparazzi,* a movie he produced in 2004.

Proximity to power, while being very far from a guarantee, does help increase those razor-thin odds. By that same logic, if you can spend time with people with a lot of disposable income who just might be excited about investing in a movie, that too greatly increases your chances. Go to the country club, hang out at Fortune 500 companies and expensive charity fundraisers, or spend more time in the affluent part of town or wherever else you have an "in" that provides a proximity to potential investors. You must figure out whatever means you have to increase your odds to meet potential investors.

While raising the money for my second movie, we reached a point at which we had obtained about half the funds and were worried we would not be able to get the other half. Fortuitously, one of the actors attached to the project met someone interested in investing while sitting front row at a mixed martial arts fight—proving that proximity to power really does matter. You are far more likely to find a potential film investor in floor seats than sitting in the nosebleed section. Your job is to make that proximity happen and up those odds.

And when you're in the right place, you have to be ready to make use of your opportunity: to oh-so-casually go into what they do not even realize is your sales pitch. Which leads us to our next *Fuck-Up*...

Key Points

- You cannot count on financing (or anything) coming to you, you have to go out and get it.
- Family members are the most common financiers for first-timers.
- The closer you can get to money, the more likely you are to obtain money.
- Always be ready to pitch; you never know when the opportunity will present itself.

Fuck-Up #7

"Selling Is about Sales"

How to make an effective pitch to potential investors

"Sell to their needs, not yours."[2]
—Earl G. Graves

The Fuck-Up…

A good sales pitch feels very little like a sales pitch. At its heart, it is not about raising money. It's not even about you or the movie. It's about the investors—their interests, their excitement, and their money.

Not having a persuasive pitch is a surefire way to fuck up your chances of making a movie before you even truly start. You might not get too many opportunities to make the pitch that will make or break your film, so make sure you approach it right.

How to Do It Right…

When approaching a potential angel investor, someone truly capable of cutting the big check to get the dream rolling, keep in mind that most people already know that investing in a movie is an extremely high-risk venture. The fact that many films lose money is not a secret. Thus, telling potential investors that this is a surefire slam-dunk of an investment is most likely going to scream "bullshit!"

THE LINGO

Angel investor: A key investor in a project, especially in its early stages.

Nevertheless, most film investors would naturally still prefer to make money than lose it. And at the very least, should a worst-case scenario occur, they'd prefer to lose as little as possible. Potential investors will appreciate it if your film has that goal in mind as well. You must separate yourself from the pack of movies that will never make money by showing potential investors why this project is different, how you've minimized the risk, and how you've increased their chances for profitability.

Many filmmakers make movies with the goal of awards, professional exposure, personal expression, or the desire to bring an issue to life. All these are wonderful motivations, but filmmaking is a business in addition to its other roles, and that can never be discounted. Whatever additional goals your film has, the potential for profitability is always going to be welcomed by would-be financiers.

It's on you to make a film that has a chance to be profitable and to show your investors this potential. That means setting out to make a movie that has commercial potential, perhaps has some commercially viable actors in it, and utilizes programs such as tax incentives to reduce the financial risk (discussed more in *Fuck-Up #12: "I Don't Care about Tax Incentives"*).

However, setting out to make a profitable film, while immensely helpful, is still not what is most likely to make people invest in a film. Most independent films get financed because they are sexy investments. That's right, "sexy investments." Most investing, while arguably more practical, is not remarkably exciting or "sexy."

THE LINGO

Sexy investment: An investment that is being made not for its potential monetary return, but primarily because of the investment's excitement.

You are looking for people who find the prospect of investing in a movie, of seeing their name roll by in the credits, or boasting to their friends and family that they are involved in a movie as, well, sexy. It's your job to make film investing sexy, exciting, or whatever other adjective appeals to them. And the truth is, they're right; investing in a movie is quite exciting and, from an investor's point of view, that is the main reason to engage in such a high-risk venture. The potential returns, both financially and otherwise, are just as high.

The key is to tailor the pitch to the individual and adapt on the fly. The best pitch masters find that little spark of excitement in the room and turn it into a wildfire. That spark is whatever gets your potential investors actually listening to you instead of dozing off. If celebrities, sex, violence, car chases, panda bears, the homeless, exotic locations, blood, techno gadgetry, wildebeests, classic novels, humor, or anything else at all seems to get them the least bit excited, then find that thing and exploit it! The spark always exists. *Everyone is excited by something or someone*, and you must find that thing that relates best to your film and light a fire of enthusiasm with it.

Perhaps investors would be excited by some screen time? Then ask yourself how much their money is worth in proportion to their (more than likely) lack of acting ability. Do they love violence, sex, romance, kittens, or ninjas? Well, then, how much are you willing to tailor your movie toward that or get them excited by whatever your movie already has that they enjoy? Are they socially conscious? Then does your movie shine light on an important social issue? Are they patrons of the arts? Well, then, can you sell your movie as the masterful work of art that it is bound to be? Ed Wood financed several films by pretending they would have religious themes and getting money from Christian groups. (He also had to stick some of the church members in parts, but fortunately for Ed, most of the acting in his films was so terrible that they fit right in.) All these ideas are interesting approaches (albeit some more morally dubious than others), so get creative and remember "any way possible (that you are morally comfortable with)" is the right answer.

Not only is everyone excited by something, better yet, everyone likes to be excited! We all want to be passionate and love what we do. And we all want to work with passionate people out of the hope that their passion will inspire that same wonderful feeling within ourselves. If you are not excited about your movie, how the hell are you going to get anyone else excited? If you really believe in a project, then this part is easy. You don't have to lie or be "selly"; you just have to let your very sincere passion shine through. Make that passion genuine, inspiring, and best of all, contagious. Your potential investors should leave the room thinking, "Wow, this is exciting. I want to be a part of this!"

If your investors are interested, quit while you're ahead. The best pitches are often the ones that involve the least talking and the most listening. If your investors are busy telling you what excites them, they are doing all the hard work for you! Your job becomes, simply, to passionately agree. The truth is, most people love to talk, and they just want a good audience to listen. If you can get your potential investors talking about their own love of movies, your task is just to affirm that this is that movie they are talking about. However, if you are doing all the talking, it can be difficult to tell whether or not the pitch is even going well. On the other hand, if you're doing all the listening, it will be crystal clear by what the other person is saying if it is going well or if you should adapt your approach.

No matter what, even if the pitch is going badly, never sound desperate. Desperation scares people off. We all want to associate ourselves with success, especially when the financial stakes are high. Desperation may make your friends and family take pity on you, but for most investors, it is an instant sign that this is something to flee.

If you do go the friends-and-family route when looking for investors, remember this opportunity is an investment, NOT a donation. You are not asking for a gift; you're asking for an investment in your movie. You are going to work hard to make them a return on that investment. Which is why, once again, your odds of raising the money are much stronger if you set out to make a profitable film.

Keep in mind that financing your movie may involve multiple investors. If you have 10 people who can give 10 percent of your budget, you are just as set. I would advise you to take what you can get wherever you can get it and pray it adds up. This approach may require a lot of legwork, but fundraising is just the beginning of your sweat equity. If you don't have enough of that key word, "passion," to do it, perhaps you've picked the wrong project and should pursue something else that you are passionate enough to see through.

> **THE LINGO**
> **Sweat equity:** An investment of someone's time and hard work, rather than money.
>
> Example: It takes a lot of sweat equity to make a passion project.

And, if you do have the passion and still want to push forward, there is one trump card that, in the entire history of making movies, has always gotten the people holding the purse strings the most excited: celebrities. Which once again leads us to our next *Fuck-Up…*

Key Points

- Pitching is about the buyer, not the seller.
- Most people know film is a very risky investment.
- Separate yourself from the pack by setting out to make a movie that is designed to have a high chance at profitability.
- Film investment should be exciting.
- Tailor your pitch to every person you pitch to.
- Always be ready to adapt your pitch on the fly.
- Find a spark of excitement and turn it into a wildfire.
- The best pitches involve the least talking and the most listening.
- If you're doing well, quit while ahead.
- The most exciting part of making films is often the celebrities involved.

Fuck-Up #8

"First, I'll Get Actors; Then I'll Get Money"

How to play the "Actors and Money" chicken-and-egg game

"Faith is taking the first step even when you don't see the whole staircase."[3]
—Martin Luther King, Jr.

The Fuck-Up...

How do you get money? Have stars.

How do you get stars? Have money.

The chicken-and-egg game as to which comes first, financing or stars, is a tricky conundrum that must be played carefully. Where most people fuck up is thinking that it's an all-or-nothing deal.

How to Do It Right…

Unlike the chicken and the egg, getting stars and money does not have to be an all-or-nothing deal. The key is to keep progressing in steps. You can raise some money to help get a star attached to your project, use that star's celebrity to raise some more money or to get another star attached, then use that to get to your next step, and so on until your project comes together.

As a first step, having some financing prior to pursuing talent will help immensely. Too much material crosses agents' and actors' desks for them to bother paying attention to a movie with zero dollars in the bank. Your project may be particularly wonderful, but unless you have an incredible connection, it is unlikely to get taken seriously when coming from an unknown with no money. This is due to the fact that there are so many people who merely *talk* about making movies that will never see that dream through. You must separate yourself from that pack. Having raised some money provides evidence that you are someone who might be able to do more than just talk. Quentin Tarantino made James Woods five offers for a part in *Reservoir Dogs,* but James never heard about any of them because his agent thought the money wasn't real, so he didn't bother telling his client about the movie. Woods later fired his agent for that mistake, but that was well after the film had already been shot—without Woods in it.

> **THE LINGO**
>
> **Talent:** Actors and other performers who appear on-screen. (This term should not be taken remotely as an insult to the many other talented artisans and craftspeople involved in the filmmaking process.)
>
> **Name talent:** Actors and other performers with enough fame that the general populace can recognize them by name.
>
> Examples: Big Bird, Rush Limbaugh, and Mario Lopez could all loosely be described as "name talent."

You may decide that you do not want, or need, name talent in your film. Many successful films have been produced without the involvement of any name talent, and this is certainly an approach worth seriously considering. Nevertheless, potential investors are likely to be more inclined to invest in a movie with recognizable actors in it, and even more inclined if those actors are particularly famous. Remember, getting investors is about playing the "chicken-and-egg" talent and money game, so you have to get chickens that are likely to lay eggs.

To a very large degree, investors are completely justified in their desire to see stars on the screen. When you reach the distribution stage, you will quickly realize that the first question you'll be asked is not "Is the movie any good?" but rather "Who's in it?" A great movie with no recognizable talent will have a much more difficult time getting a wide audience to see it than even a mediocre movie with some recognizable faces in it. And if nobody is going to bother watching your film, nobody is going to have a chance to discover just how good it truly is. Furthermore, associating with famous people is potentially what your investors will find to be one of the most enticing parts of being involved in a movie.

Key Points

- Getting money and talent is a chicken-and-egg game, but you don't need all of one to get the other. You can work in steps as you continue to make progress.
- Having raised some money before approaching talent sets you ahead of the pack.
- Casting famous people is what is most likely to get your investors excited. It is also to a large extent what helps determine if your movie gets seen and has an opportunity at success.

Fuck-Up #9

"No Stars Will Want to Be in My Movie"

How to brainstorm stars you really can attach

"Strip away the phony tinsel of Hollywood and you'll find the real tinsel underneath."[4]

—Oscar Levant

The Fuck-Up...

To many would-be filmmakers, the world of celebrities seems like an impossible fortress to break into. It's a world built of tinsel, smoke, and mirrors designed by gatekeepers to appear impenetrable to outsiders. Although many gatekeepers work hard to maintain that appearance, when it is demystified, we realize that it is not always quite as impenetrable as it may appear.

How to Do It Right...

Because the world of celebrities is filled with gatekeepers, how do you go about attaching a recognizable face that's going to get your investors excited and lead you to box office gold? The short answer is once

THE LINGO
Gatekeepers: People who make a living representing the interests of their clients.
Examples: Agents, managers, lawyers, publicists, and assistants all frequently function as gatekeepers.

again "any way possible (that you feel morally comfortable with)." If you can beg, plead, or sneak your way into a talent attachment, great! Harvey Keitel got involved in *Reservoir Dogs* through the wife of producer Lawrence Bender's acting teacher. The filmmakers landed not only a great actor, but also an energetic producer to boot. Harvey was so enthusiastic about the script that he helped raise the budget from $30,000 to $1.5 million.

Anything you are morally comfortable with that has a chance of working is a good approach. And if that doesn't work, there is another golden rule I am almost as fond of as "any way possible," and that is "it can't hurt to try."

Currently, I am guessing Tom Cruise is not starring in your movie. And should you call Tom Cruise's agent, the worst-case scenario is that after that phone call, Tom Cruise is still not starring in your movie. Nothing has changed (besides that you have attempted *Mission Impossible* on your own) and you haven't lost anything, so why the hell not try?

Naturally, there are more realistic potential names than Tom Cruise, but the theory remains the same no matter where you're aiming. I once heard Joel Schumacher say to a group of students, "I'm jealous of you. You have no reputation to ruin." If you are just starting out, you might as well put yourself out there and try. You really do have little to lose early in your career, and it may even prove more possible than you think—if done properly.

There are some good techniques to go about brainstorming names and faces that might actually be interested in being a part of your project.

One good approach is to think about recognizable faces that may be looking for interesting opportunities. A TV actor who has yet to carry a movie might be very excited to take on a film role. A supporting actor who has yet to be the lead might relish such an opportunity. A still recognizable face that has hit a dry spell might be happy to have you knock a little dust off her career. The rehab regular might think you are just the chance he needs to prove he can stay sober long enough to get a movie "in the can." These are all great approaches and should be how you think about what actors you would like to attach: who is "attainable"?

> **THE LINGO**
>
> **In the can:** A term meaning something has been filmed. (The expression comes from working with celluloid film. After it is shot, it goes back into a can to avoid exposure to light. The term is now used whether or not you're shooting on film to imply something has been shot.)
>
> Example: We have two scenes in the can already and one still left to shoot today.

I encourage you to aim high and then work your way down the list, so to speak. If you want to start with Tom Cruise, then go for it. I recommend beginning somewhere around "attainable but a reach." Think of this technique like applying for colleges: most applicants have their dream schools and then their safeties. The only difference is, you can't send out a bunch of applications at once. The industry standard is to make one offer per part at a time, and breaking that rule is a good way to ruin the reputation you've yet to build.

When you have your list, start with your top choice first and work your way down should you get rejected. Who knows, fairy tales do happen. And if this offer doesn't work out, at least you'll know you tried, and you can keep racking your brain for that recognizable face your investors will know and that you can potentially get. However, on a side note, never tell an actor she is anything but your first choice—no reason to hurt anyone's feelings.

When you do have some names in mind, how do you get these actors excited? Chances are, they are not doing a "little movie" for what is to them its "little paycheck." Some actors simply love to work, and finding a known actor with some free time on his hands might be all you need— but it might take more than that.

Fortunately, for independent filmmakers, many actors love saying, "I'm working on this little indie." The reason this is so trendy is that the assumption is that "little indies" will have more interesting roles than bigger budget movies. Your goal is to make sure that statement is true. Having great parts that actors can sink their teeth into and test their craft is a huge advantage. It is your job to convince them that with your film they'll get to play just such a role.

A "great part" often means having an interesting character that challenges an actor. It may also be a part that helps an actor branch out into new territory. Casting against type is a great way to excite an actor who otherwise would not touch a film of your budget size with a 10-foot pole. A well-known supporting actor is going to relish the chance to prove he's leading man material. A starlet known for her beauty might like something that shows she has the acting chops to go with the eye-candy body. Conversely, someone known for conservative family-friendly fair might love an opportunity to show his dangerous side. Keep this in mind when thinking about your casting options. Too often, people merely imagine actors who are known for playing characters similar to the ones you want them to play in your movie; it's exciting to break that mold.

With that said, casting for type is also a perfectly valid approach. Casting a horror cult icon is going to be a lot more appealing to his or her loyal fans if your movie is, in fact, a horror film. Consider who appeals to your built-in audience—and don't be limited to just actors. A lot of people who are not famous for acting would cherish the opportunity to get in front of the camera. This can work especially well if their celebrity relates to your movie's subject matter. If your film is about a sport, why not see whether you can involve an athlete famous in that sport? If your film involves a death metal band, break dancing, unicycle riding, or whatever, figure out who's famous for doing that. After you've brainstormed who it is you want in your movie, it's time to go get them, and that leads us to our next *Fuck-Up*…

Key Points

- There is no one right way to get name talent. Any way possible (that you feel comfortable with) is the right way. Make your own rules.
- It's okay to aim high first and then work your way down.
- Brainstorm what actors are worthwhile and attainable.
- You have to get actors excited, and that means having great parts that challenge them or provide them with a new opportunity.
- Try to cast for or against type, whichever is more likely to excite the individuals you're going after.
- Celebrity attachments are not always professional actors.

Fuck-Up #10

"Stars Will Want to Be in My Movie"

How to really go about getting stars

"Even a fool knows you can't touch the stars, but it won't keep the wise from trying."[5]
—Harry Anderson

The Fuck-Up...

Assuming that a particular star will want to be in your movie is just as common a mistake as assuming that *no* stars will want to be in your movie.

New filmmakers frequently think, "Surely, recognizable actors, musicians, and celebrities will want to be a part of my incredible project, right?" But the truth is, more often than not, this sort of genuine enthusiasm gets dealt a very empty plate of reality. However, should you approach the process of pursuing talent with a practical plan that is able to adapt to its obstacles, you might end up with a better cast than even the dreamers dreamt possible.

How to Do It Right...

Let's say you have some great ideas for attainable names and/or faces, but have no clue how to get in touch with them. I have good news for you: there is a roadmap for that. One that you can go about yourself—or one you can attach a casting director (C.D.) or producer to help navigate. Let's discuss all three of those options.

Casting Directors

When you're considering attaching a casting director at the early stages of the talent and money "chicken-and-egg" game, it's important to get a good one—with a track record. As we discussed in *Fuck-Up #8: "First, I'll Get Actors; Then I'll Get Money,"* a lot of projects pass an agent's desk daily, so you need to separate yourself from that pack. Good casting directors have relationships with agents and managers they can utilize to help your project get their attention. After all, it's in an agent's best interest to keep the casting directors they work with happy, because casting directors are the buyers of the product that agents sell: actors.

An established casting director instantly gives your project added legitimacy. Even if you don't have a long track record, you can take advantage of your casting director's. Naturally, that advantage will likely come at a price, and you will have to pay a casting director part of her fee to be involved in a project at an early stage; that is another reason having some money in place as a first step is immensely helpful. Few established casting directors would work on a project out of the mere hope it'll get to a place where they can make some money later. They've been around long enough to see enough movies fail and likely know better. If you have raised a little money, using it to attach a casting director is an idea worth seriously considering.

Casting directors are also great at helping you brainstorm potential talent attachments. One of the great benefits of using good C.D.s is they are a veritable encyclopedia of actors and are very good at coming up with potential names that might work for your project. Often they can tell you who is looking for work, what type of work, and who is just after a big paycheck. In other words, they can help you focus your search and avoid wasting a lot of time chasing dead ends.

Casting directors can be found by consulting other filmmakers for recommendations or by using production guides. (LA411.com, NewYork411.com, and NYPG.com are a few popular online production guides.) You can also use IMDB.com to find out who has cast movies similar in size and genre to your film to figure out who might be a good fit for your project. IMDBPro.com (which is a pay service) will often provide their direct contact info.

> **THE LINGO**
>
> **Production guide:** An encyclopedia of film crew, services, and vendors in a particular region. (In the old days, these were books, but now they're mostly online databases.)

However, if you are not ready to take on a casting director, contacting agents and managers is absolutely something you or your producer can do on your own.

Producers

In the Hollywood system, the headlining stars of a movie are rarely attached by casting directors. Because attaching stars is key to the early stages of packaging a film, the film's producers often do this job themselves. For independent films, it can go either way: a casting director may help attach a film's stars, or a capable producer can be equally effective.

> **THE LINGO**
>
> **Packaging:** Putting together the principal elements of a film, such as its screenplay, stars, director, producer(s), and financing.

When you're considering attaching a producer to help you pursue talent, many of the same rules apply as when considering a casting director. It'll help immensely if your producer has a good track record and industry relationships. Once again, this will help separate you from the pack and give your project added legitimacy.

To get an experienced producer, you may have to pay part of their fee up front and/or guarantee him continued involvement in the film. Often a name producer may end up coming on board a project only "in name" and may or may not be a hands-on producer down the road. It can be frustrating to pay a "producer in name" while someone else does most of the work. However, if that name is likely to be what gets the ball rolling for your movie, this approach is still worth considering.

> **THE LINGO**
>
> **Producer in name:** Someone who lends his name and reputation to a project but will not be working on it much beyond that.

If attaching an experienced casting director or producer isn't an option for you, a DIY approach to pursuing talent is also completely acceptable.

DIY Talent Attachment

Finding out what agent or manager represents an actor is fairly easy. You can look up this information on pay websites such as IMDBPro.com or WhoRepresents.com. The Screen Actors Guild also provides a free "actors to locate" service that you can call (1-800-503-6737), and it will tell you whom SAG has listed as an actor's representative. This service rarely gives a specific agent's name but rather the name of the agency where that actor's agent works. Simply call the agency and ask the receptionist who is the agent for the actor you're seeking. The receptionist can then transfer you to that agent's "desk."

> **THE LINGO**
>
> **Desk:** A word for someone's assistant, used due to the high turnover of assistants who may be "covering the desk" at any moment.
>
> Example: "I'll transfer you to Joe's desk, and by that I mean his assistant."

Getting in touch with the agent, manager, or more likely his assistant is the easy step. Getting past these people and to the actor is the real challenge. Being a gatekeeper is part of an agent's and a manager's job, so you have to convince them to want to help you. Unlike actors, they are far less likely to be excited about the juiciness of a part. There are some agents who don't just care about the money and are working hard to find their clients good parts. These rare agents are wonderful, and should you encounter them, consider yourself fortunate. However, most care primarily about the money. So when they inevitably ask you to "send over the offer" (which means email), the first thing they will look at is how much you are offering their client and, in turn, them. Agents make their living by taking 10 percent of their clients' fees ("managers" can take more), so if the client is not getting paid well, neither are they.

> **THE LINGO**
>
> **Representation:** Agents, managers, publicists, lawyers, business managers, and various other people who make their living as gatekeepers and consul.

If you cannot get agents worked up over how much money they will make, you have to appeal to why this is a good project for their client. The important point to remember (and to sometimes remind agents) is that they work for their clients, not the other way around. Explain why it would be a remarkably good idea for their client to do this project and how grateful their client will be to them for having found this gem. Then go off and pray that it just so happens the actor you want has been nagging her agent or manager to find her an indie/drama/romance/socially conscious political thriller about killer bridesmaids, or whatever it is you're offering up.

It is highly probable that you will not even get an agent on the phone initially. If you *do* get the agent on the phone, by all means seize that moment and sell, sell, sell! 'Cause, hey, that's what agents do for a living themselves, so give them a good taste of their own medicine. Take that opportunity to convince the agent that your movie is the best possible career move his client can make. However, the more likely outcome is that you get an assistant on the phone in lieu of the actual agent. As anyone in the industry knows, assistants are true gatekeepers as well. Befriending an assistant can open up magical doors that can lead you to a fantastic Hollywood world, like stepping through the wardrobe into Narnia. Assistants decide what messages the agent gets, what phone calls he actually returns, in what order he returns them, and often, what information the agent hears about each project. I cannot encourage you enough to be nice and, yes, even befriend assistants if you can. Always remember the assistants' names because they are absolutely power brokers in their own right.

When you have an assistant on the phone, the first step in the process is to "check avail," which means to check the actor's availability for the dates you want. If an actor is not available, you can either change your shooting dates or move to another actor on your list. If an actor is available for your date, the assistant will ask you to "send the offer." Compose a professional email that includes:

- Name of the actor the offer is for (put this in the email subject line).
- Title of the movie.
- Production company making the movie.
- Short synopsis of the movie (of course, tailored to make their client's role sound the best).
- Short synopsis of the part you're offering (of course, tailored to excite their particular client).
- Shooting dates. This can be a range if you are not completely certain (for example, five weeks between January 17 and February 28).
- The movie's total budget.
- How much money you're offering the client. This amount is normally worded in terms of pay per week (X dollars per week for Y number of weeks).

Throwing Money at an Actor

If you cannot attach an actor solely on the strength of the part or the coolness of your indie film, perhaps throwing money at her is not a bad approach. If making an actor a juicy monetary offer is what it takes to get your financing ball rolling, that one big blow to your wallet may very well be worth the expense. If you can afford to make an offer that will actually make the agent take the time to hand his client your script, go for it. If it is a choice between paying an actor a good chunk of your budget and having no movie at all, the choice is easy.

Many independent films spend one-fourth to one-third of their budget on the talent. Studio films often spend much more than that. When figuring out how much money you can afford to throw at an actor, be aware that you may be setting a contractual precedent thanks to a legal clause known as "favored nations." "Favored nations" doesn't refer to anyone on the

General Counsel of the United Nations (unless Mexico does acting gigs on the side). If an actor gets a favored nations clause in her contract, it means she is guaranteed that no other actor will get better terms than she does. For example, let's say you sign up Actor A to do your movie for $1. Then down the road you contract Actor B for $10,000. Well, guess what? If Actor A had a "favored nations" clause in her contract, then her rate just went up $10,000 as well because it guarantees no one will get paid more than her. If you have

> **THE LINGO**
>
> **Favored nations clause:** A contractual term guaranteeing the contracting party will receive terms on par with other parties' contracts. This could be in reference to salary, profit participation, or anything else specified.

two, three, or more parts for which you intend to go after actors of relatively the same fame, there is a more than likely chance they all will demand favored nations clauses in their contracts to assure they get paid as well as their peers. Thus, when deciding what type of money to throw at an actor, you should calculate what you can afford to pay all the actors who are likely to insist upon a favored nations clause and divide accordingly.

Key Points

- Talent can be attached by producers or casting directors.
- Agents and managers exist to serve as gatekeepers to their clients.
- Resources such as IMDBPro.com can tell you who represents an actor.
- You will often end up talking to assistants. Be nice to them. They are the gatekeeper's gatekeepers and powerbrokers in their own right.
- Getting past the agent and to the client is the real goal.
- Agents and managers primarily care about money.
- You have to sell agents and managers on why their client will be grateful they brought him this project.
- Throwing money at an actor is often a valid approach.
- How much money you pay one actor may set a legal precedent for how much you'll have to pay other stars.

Fuck-Up #11

"My Actors Are Committed"

How to know if your talent is attached "enough"

"A verbal contract isn't worth the paper it's printed on."[6]
—Samuel Goldwyn

The Fuck-Up...

So you know a guy who says he knows a guy who says he can get a famous guy to be in your movie? Sadly, more often than not, loose connections don't pan out, and it may take more than your word to convince investors someone famous is interested in doing your movie. While you do not need a signed contract to begin leveraging a celebrity's interest into raising money, a sign of commitment does help.

How to Do It Right...

If you are early in the financing stages of a project, you may want to consider seeking what is called a "letter of intent" (also sometimes called a "letter of interest," or "LOI" for short) from name talent. What this letter means is that the person signing is in no way, shape, or form actually legally "attached" to do your movie, but rather that he is interested should you actually get the money and pull this thing together.

> **THE LINGO**
>
> **Attachment:** Elements such as actors, directors, or anyone else who is committed to being part of a project.

LOIs exist to show potential investors proof that these actors really are interested in a project—should the money come together. LOIs are less binding and also less expensive than contractual attachments. More binding attachments for name actors frequently involve "pay-or-play" deals. A pay-or-play deal means that if the movie gets made, you must pay the actor, AND if the movie does not get made, you must still pay the actor. The theory behind this deal is that the actor is blocking out dates for you, and thus you are potentially costing her other work. So she is going to get paid for blocking out that time no matter what.

> **THE LINGO**
>
> **Pay or play:** A contract provision that commits compensation for a project whether or not that project ever goes into production.

Denzel Washington had a $20 million pay-or-play deal on *American Gangster* when Antoine Fuqua was attached to direct it. That project fell apart, and Washington got his $20 million without having to make the movie. Later, when Ridley Scott got attached to the same film, the producers made Denzel another $20 million pay-or-play deal. This time the movie got made, but the payday was still the same. In total, $40 million for Mr. Washington on that one movie!

If you cannot afford a monetary commitment early in the financing stages, seek an LOI. The truth is these letters rarely obligate people to do absolutely anything. Wording such as "subject to availability" and "conditions of terms" always gives them an out should they change their minds later. Although the letter is noncommittal in nature, it still shows their interest and puts you in a much better place for approaching potential investors. This is a great way to keep the ball rolling forward on a project. Often, just finding out an actor is aware of the project and might do it can be incredibly exciting to investors.

New filmmakers are sometimes so desperate to attach anyone to their projects that they forget it's not enough for an actor to excite *them*. If a particular actor's interest doesn't excite potential investors, it's not going to help you raise money. Ten LOIs from very minor celebrities are simply not as valuable as one letter from someone more recognizable. Remember, the goal isn't just to seek out attachments; it is to seek out attachments that will excite potential investors—to get actor "chickens" that will help lay money "eggs."

Key Points

- Letters of intent are helpful financing tools that prove there is actor interest in your movie.
- LOIs are noncommittal in nature.
- Contracts often require expensive commitments.
- The bigger the talent you can get to sign an LOI, the more excited your potential investors will likely be.

Fuck-Up #12

"I Don't Care about Tax Incentives"

Why you should love tax credits

"There may be liberty and justice for all, but there are tax breaks only for some."[7]
—Martin A. Sullivan

The Fuck-Up...

If someone came up and offered you 10 to 50 percent of the funds for your movie, would you take it? Unfortunately, many new filmmakers wind up missing out on money for their film purely because "taxes" and thereby "tax incentives" sound boring or intimidating and they don't want to deal with that.

I promise you that once you understand a little bit about tax incentives, you will agree they are perhaps the most exciting part of filmmaking there is. A tremendous mistake many first-time film-makers make is either being unaware of how great tax incentives truly are or, worse yet, simply not bothering to utilize them.

How to Do It Right...

Tax incentives are so valuable that it has become increasingly rare for any film, independent or studio, to go into production without taking advantage of some tax-incentive program—regardless of where the movie is actually supposed to take place. *Detroit Rock City* was actually shot in Toronto, *Fast Five* took place in Rio de Janeiro but was filmed mostly in Puerto Rico, and Jackie Chan's *Rumble in the Bronx* has mountains behind the New York City skyline because the film was shot entirely in Vancouver. If there is any way for your film to make use of a good tax incentive, the smart move is to utilize one to the fullest extent possible.

Money from tax credits can be used to help finance your film, pay back your investors, or a combination of the two. Tax credits vary state by state, region by region, and country by country. At the time I am writing this, the state of Connecticut has a 30 percent credit; New York, 30 percent (with an extra 5 percent if you are in New York City); Missouri, 35 percent; Puerto Rico, 40 percent; Michigan, 42 percent; and numerous other states, cities, and countries have similar credits to varying degrees. Tax credits change frequently, and some have likely already changed between the time it took me to write this and you to read it. Furthermore, the rules as to what expenses are applicable and how the credits are paid out also vary and change. So a little home-work will be necessary for you to figure out what region has the best incentives for your project, but trust me, as you're about to discover, it's more than worth the effort.

You can research tax-incentive programs online or by contacting the film commission in the location you're thinking about shooting (in some places where there is no film commission, this duty often falls to the business or tourism office). Most commissions have a website, and you can also find sites that'll compare up-to-date information about different regions' incentives (try to make sure you're looking at an up to date listing because tax incentives often change).

Types of tax incentives vary greatly, but the most common are:

- **Refundable Credits:** This involves getting a check directly from the state. When you file the tax return for your business (the one created to make your movie), your movie will receive a credit based on a percentage of all the expenses that qualify.

If your movie owes a lot in taxes, that credit will reduce what it owes. More likely, the credit will be worth a lot more than your movie owes in taxes, so you'll get a refund check. That's real money your movie can use.

- **Transferable Credits:** Unlike refundable credits, these credits can be used only to offset tax liability and cannot result in a refund check directly from the state. However, what you can do is sell the credit to another business or individual and let them use the credit to reduce what they owe in taxes. So the sale is how you turn the credit into real money your movie can use. Generally, you'll have to sell the credit for less than its value to make the purchase appealing to the buyer.
- **Nonrefundable and Nontransferable Credits:** These credits cannot result in a refund check from the state, and you cannot sell them. Your movie can use these credits only to offset tax money it owes to the state. These are generally the least appealing kind of tax credits.
- **Rebates:** The government sets aside money to give out based on qualified expenditures. That money is paid directly to production companies based on a percentage of qualified expenditures.

Let's take a further look at why tax incentives are such an incredible help to filmmakers. We'll utilize a make-believe $100 movie (I've yet to see the feature film that actually costs only $100, but it does make the math easy, so go with it for now). The tax incentive will be given only on money spent in the region where the incentive is offered. So if you're taking advantage of a New Mexico tax credit but casting out of L.A., you will not receive any credit for the money spent in L.A. Thus, where you can, you should make every possible effort to have as many of your expenses eligible for the tax incentive. For example, I made a movie utilizing a Connecticut tax credit with many of the actors coming from New York. It became an important struggle to make sure all the vehicles were gassed up only in Connecticut so we could get the tax credit on the massive expense of paying for gasoline. You should apply the same philosophy and spend every dollar you can where you'll get the most back for it.

For the sake of our easy math, let's say you actually spend an approved $100 in a region with a 25 percent transferable credit. What you will get in return for spending that $100 is a certificate for $25, which can be used instead of real money to pay taxes. Because it is a "transferable" credit, the expectation is that you will sell that certificate to a company or individual. Then that buyer will use that certificate in lieu of paying that amount of money in taxes. You get actual cash only by selling the credit.

Prices vary for selling your tax credits. I have heard of sales from as high as 95 cents on the dollar to as low as 50 cents on the dollar. Having a larger tax credit to sell will generally get you a better rate. There are also firms that will combine your credit with other movies' credits and sell them in a bulk deal. Keep in mind that these companies will take a percent as their fee, so they should get you a good enough rate to make this fee worthwhile.

In this manner, you can see how a $25 credit might translate into $15 or $20 in your movie's bank account. However, for this example, our whole movie cost only $100, so getting $20 back is pretty good. It is entirely possible through tax incentives to get back 10, 20, or even 30 percent of your budget!!!

Know that when researching tax incentives, you must consider more than just types of credits and their percentages. The rules also vary region by region as to what expenses are applicable toward the incentive.

For example, at first glance, New York State's program may look more appealing than Connecticut's. However, upon closer inspection, you will realize that Connecticut's program allows you to claim above-the-line expenses toward your credit, whereas New York's does not. Because above-the-line expenses (such as the director, star actors, producers, and the script) can frequently be as much as 30 to 50 percent of your budget, this can be a huge loss. Therefore, New York's programs may be more appealing to projects with a relatively small above-the-line budget, and Connecticut's may be more appealing if you have a heavy above-the-line. Another important difference is that Connecticut currently requires only a rough cut of your film before it begins processing your credit, whereas New York's program requires your film to be 100 percent complete. Thus, Connecticut is likely to get you your credit quicker, which is crucial if you need the money to actually finish your film.

Rules also vary regarding local hires, local sound stage usage, and other applicable expenses. Some states even have regulations regarding content, so if your project is particularly gruesome or controversial, that can become an issue. I know of at least one film rejected for a tax incentive because the state of Michigan didn't want to be seen as encouraging the cannibalistic eating of children, which is what that film was about.

The pros and cons of different incentives should be explored as they pertain to your project, but no matter what, they should definitely be explored! Most of the time, surprisingly friendly people staff the offices that run these programs. This is because it is their job to attract productions to their respective regions. So let these friendly folks help you understand their programs better. If there is a location or locations you are thinking about shooting in, research the tax-incentive programs, and do so as early as possible to make sure you get your paperwork in before you miss any deadlines or the rules change. Should you discover that the place you are thinking about making your movie does not have a good tax-incentive program, I strongly encourage you to consider shooting someplace else.

Key Points

- Tax incentives are wonderful.
- You should try very hard to shoot in the area with the best tax incentives that your project will allow.
- Tax credits, their percentages, and their rules vary by region and change frequently. Do your homework.
- A 25 percent tax credit will *not* necessarily translate into 25 percent of your budget.
- Tax credits can help finance your film.
- Tax credits can help pay back your investors.
- If the place you're thinking about shooting does not have good tax incentives, think about shooting someplace else.

Fuck-Up #13

"If I Can't Raise All the Money, I Can't Start My Movie"

How to make your movie, even without all the money raised

> "I have never been in a situation where having money made it worse."[8]
> —Clinton Jones

The Fuck-Up...

You need four legs and a top to make most tables. But what if you had only three legs and no top? Could you begin construction on your table while still working to get the missing pieces? The answer is, of course, yes.

Many would-be filmmakers assume they can't start making their movie until they raise all the necessary funds. This is completely wrong. Films frequently begin shooting without raising the entirety of their budgets up front. The question is, how do you make sure you don't end up with a movie that's as useless as a three-legged table with no top?

How to Do It Right...

In addition to tax credits (discussed in *Fuck-Up #12: "I Don't Care about Tax Incentives"*), there are many ways to make your movie with only part of the money initially in hand. In fact, a lot of movies knowingly go into production without having raised all the financing they're going to need. Director Sofia Coppola said her famous father, Francis Ford Coppola, advised her that, "Even if you're just starting and you don't have any money, just go ahead and it will all fall in."[9] And thus she set out to make *Lost in Translation* without all the financing in place. She continued exhaustively fundraising all during shooting, somehow pulled everything together, and the film went on to receive four Oscar nominations and one win.

Although I would not suggest entering production flat broke, going in with enough money to shoot the movie but not to actually finish editing can, in many cases, work. Some successful movies have even been shot intermittently, spending months and years in hiatus while funds were raised to shoot the next part. John Waters shot *Pink Flamingos* only on weekends so that he could spend weekdays trying to find financing to keep the movie going week to week. Peter Jackson made his first feature film *Bad Taste* shooting on various weekends over a four-year period, using friends for his cast. These are impressive feats, which run the very real risk of the movie dragging on and never being completed at all. Both making a film and fundraising are incredibly difficult tasks individually and become exponentially more exhausting when combined. Nevertheless, if this is the only way to get your movie made, and you're willing to make the sacrifices necessary, the choice is easy.

If you decide to use this common, albeit risky approach, there are several means of raising money as you go. You may be able to show off your best dailies to help excite potential investors. If you are financed through production but not post-production, you can put together a "rough cut" of your film that is hopefully good enough to show around as a tool to help raise the money to finish the movie. Alternatively, you can also use some of the footage you've shot to make a "trailer" and use it in the same manner to show potential investors what you're up to. Often if investors feel as though a movie is already happening, with or without them, it will make them want to get on board rather than risk missing out on something truly exciting.

> **THE LINGO**
>
> **Dailies:** The raw unedited footage of each day's work. In the case of film, rushed from the lab "daily."
>
> **Rough cut:** An early edit of a movie that shows the story fully assembled although not finalized.

Starting with as much money already raised as possible is going to be helpful, and starting near broke is more than likely to be a complete and utter disaster. However, if you reach a point where you are tired of *not* making your movie, there's a lot to be said for gaining the momentum of starting production—no matter what. Then keep fighting and always make the most of what you do have at every step of the process.

> ## Key Points
> - You don't have to have your entire budget raised to start making your movie.
> - Lots of movies raise money as they go.
> - It's possible to make a film piece by piece as you gather the cash.
> - You can show potential investors your partially completed movie to try to raise more cash.
> - The more money you have already raised, the better off you are.

Fuck-Up #14

"There's No Harm in Getting Creative with My Financing"

The reality of credit cards, pre-sales, negative pick-ups, and gap financing

> "There's no such thing as a free lunch."[10]
> —Milton Friedman

The Fuck-Up...

In the desperation to make a movie, many filmmakers will take any road, no matter how treacherous, that whispers promises of leading them toward their goal. Although getting a movie financed is always a tremendous destination to reach, certain paths have cautionary signs to be wary of.

How to Do It Right...

Credit Cards

Kevin Smith famously funded most of his debut film *Clerks* by maxing out several credit cards. That daring effort paid off, and Kevin went on to have an impressive career. This story is often told by filmmakers looking to emulate Smith's success by jumping into their own financial peril. But the truth is for every Kevin Smith, there are thousands of failures. Running up insane credit card debt is extremely risky; it can leave you with crushing debt that endlessly grows with the interest rate every month. Furthermore, it can ruin your credit and leave you (or whoever's credit card you're using) in a terrible financial state for the rest of your days. Long story short, if you can't afford to pay off a credit card bill in a timely manner, don't use it. This is NOT the right way to finance your movie. Luckily, there are other options....

Pre-Sales

Pre-sales are another means of raising additional money to help finance your film. In a pre-sale, you sell part or all of the distribution rights to your movie before it is finished. Many distributors are willing to buy a work in progress, sometimes well before shooting even begins. Mel Gibson's *The Passion of the Christ* relied on $10 million in international pre-sales. New Line covered almost the entire cost of *The Lord of the Rings* franchise by using international pre-sales combined with German tax shelters and New Zealand subsidies.

New filmmakers without a track record and/or a known star attached to their movie may find pre-sales difficult to come by because distributors generally want some assurance that the film will be worth the expense. The worse track record or fewer "bankable" entities involved in the film, the lower you can expect the price of a pre-sale to be. Distributors also know that if you are trying to sell early, you are most likely somewhat desperate for cash. Or worse yet, that you no longer believe the movie is any good and are simply trying to unload it before bad word of mouth gets out. Thus, as a general rule, the money you will receive for a pre-sale is less than what you could theoretically get for a quality-completed product later.

> **THE LINGO**
>
> **Bankable:** Someone or something whose involvement in a project is seen as likely to assure its financial success.

Many producers will engage solely in international pre-sales. This means selling off foreign territories (anything outside the United States and Canada). This allows producers to wait for a completed product to sell the domestic rights and some other territories, which they hope is where they will really make money. Pre-selling international territories can indeed help raise additional funds for completing a film, but should be done with caution because it can decrease a film's potential profits down the road. If you sell territories to make the movie, you can't sell those territories again to profit on them later.

Pre-sales may be viewed as unfavorable by your investors if they see the sales cutting into their potential profit margin. International sales have become a key source of revenue for many of today's movies, so eliminating this revenue source can be costly. However, some investors may prefer pre-sales as an alternative to having to dig deeper into their own pockets to cover the upfront financial risk of making the movie.

With all of that said, if the myth about pre-sales is true and you have, in fact, lost faith in the quality of your movie, a pre-sale might be a great idea. Selling your movie early may actually be more lucrative if the finished product is not any good.

Negative Pick-Ups

In a "negative pick-up" deal, a distributor agrees in advance to buy your movie when it's finished shooting (which, if you shoot on film, would be when there is a film "negative" shot, hence the term). The idea is that although the distributor is not going to give you any money until the movie is finished shooting, you can use this promise of future money to secure some type of loan or perhaps additional investment.

> **THE LINGO**
>
> **Negative:** When you're shooting on film, this is your raw stock. It is called a negative because its light and dark parts are inverted from what was filmed.

Negative pick-up deals have become less and less common in recent years, especially for films in lower budget realms. Bigger name producers with good track records can sometimes still get these deals from distributors, but it's become harder for everyone.

Negative pick-ups generally specify that the film must be delivered pursuant to certain terms, including that it be of a certain vaguely defined quality. Distributors can find many reasons why they won't have to honor such a deal by claiming your movie is in violation of a number of poorly defined requirements, so these deals often prove less helpful than you might hope. Lenders know this and thus frequently don't see a negative pick-up deal as much of a guarantee they'll get their money.

Furthermore, negative pick-up deals nearly always require a completion bond. This is like insurance on finishing a movie. The way it works is you pay a fee to a bond company and promise to deliver a film on a certain budget, certain schedule, perhaps with specified actors, and with only minor deviations from an approved script. If extraneous costs arise, the bond company is supposed to step in and help cover them. Of course, as with any insurance company, if it can find any way possible to claim you are in violation of the agreement, it will avoid payment. Read a bond carefully, and you are sure to find a laundry list of cases where the company does NOT have to pay up. Furthermore, if the bond company concludes you're in violation of the agreement, it can seize control of the movie and even decide to halt production rather than risk the cost of continuing with the movie. Many incomplete films have died an unceremonious death under a bond company's ownership. This is what happened in the case of Terry Gilliam's doomed *Man of La Mancha*. As the film hit a series of intense obstacles, the bond company ended up owning what had been shot. Gilliam spent years trying to buy the movie back from the bond company, but as of this date, he's still fighting... unsuccessfully.

Gap Financing

"Gap financing" (also called "bridge loans") is a term that was popularized in the mortgage industry. It refers to an interim loan designed to cover a period when you're waiting for additional expected money to come in.

For a movie, you can sometimes get a gap loan to cover a time period when you know that financing will be coming in later, but just not soon enough. With the popularization of tax credits, some banks now offer gap loans specifically based on the assumption they will recoup their money from the tax credit, regardless of whether or not your film ever gets sold.

A gap loan will generally offer a short-term interest rate that isn't too bad, but then skyrockets should it not be paid back in an agreed-upon time frame. Gap loans can be helpful if you're waiting for a tax credit or additional investor check to come in. However, I recommend using them only if you know with a great deal of confidence that the money really is coming before the interest rate increases and thus you can pay back the lender in a timely manner. Otherwise, the terms become heavily beneficial to the lender once the interest rate skyrockets. Sometimes the terms are so bad that you may be better off incurring credit card debt, and as we've already discussed, that's also a pretty terrible idea.

Key Points

- People will do a lot of things to get their movies financed. Think carefully before taking certain approaches.
- Credit card debt is a terrible way to finance a film.
- Pre-sales involve selling off the distribution rights for certain territories before a film is completed.
- Pre-sales can cost your movie profit it *may* have made later.
- In a negative pick-up deal, a distributor agrees in advance to buy a movie when it is completed.
- Negative pick-up deals can be hard to come by and often involve terms that allow distributors to get out of any obligations.
- Completion bonds can be very difficult to collect. Don't count on them.
- Gap financing is a type of loan that provides short-term cash, with an interest rate that skyrockets after a certain time period.
- Consider gap financing only if you're very confident you can pay it back before the rates begin to skyrocket.

Fuck-Up #15

"I Don't Need a Business Plan"
Why a business plan is crucial

"The two biggest myths about me are that I'm an intellectual, because I wear these glasses, and that I'm an artist, because my films lose money."[11]
—Woody Allen

The Fuck-Up...

A business plan is to film financing what a resume is to job hunting. While your resume alone will likely never get you a job, no one will likely take you seriously if you don't have one. So, you have to have one and it has to be impressive—the same goes for a business plan.

Some people may argue that filmmaking should be art and not business, so why would you make a business plan? Their mistake is treating the two as mutually exclusive. The earlier you realize that a film is many things, including a business, the better off you will be.

How to Do It Right...

More than likely, you are not chasing the dream of filmmaking to write business plans. And yes, a good chunk of a business plan will have zero fun or entertainment value (although it's your job to make sure there's some in it someplace). Nevertheless, it is still necessary, and you will find that the process of writing it will force you to think through your strategies and thus actually help you and your movie succeed.

It doesn't really matter if you are raising money to start a dry cleaners, Internet startup, or any other type of business; the document you give to potential investors describing what you're offering is your "business plan." It is also sometimes called an "investment memorandum," "offering memorandum," "prospectus," or "private placement memorandum" (or "P.P.M.," to pretend as though this document could be made cool by using an acronym), but any of these names means the same thing.

> ### THE LINGO
> **Business plan:** A written proposal detailing a commercial activity that is used in raising capital.
>
> Example: The business plan took six months, four lawyers, and three accountants to write it. The movie took three weeks to shoot and 85 minutes to watch.

When you approach someone to invest in a film, you are absolutely proposing a business investment, and you must conduct yourself accordingly. You are not asking for a handout, donation, or gift; you are asking for an investment. Even if you're asking your family and friends, it is still an investment because you're going to work very hard to make them a return. A movie is a high-risk investment venture and should be treated as such. Do yourself a favor and have a professional, thought-out, and enticing business plan ready to go.

You can write a business plan yourself, and it may even prove less intimidating than it sounds. There are several good books or courses you can take on how to go about writing one. The topic is more than worthy of its own book, but to give you an idea of what a business plan might entail, here are some likely sections:

To start, you might have:

- Your objective
- Company description
- Bios for the management team
- Legal disclaimers regarding investing in general
- The amount of money you're looking for
- The amount you are offering investors in priority return

> **THE LINGO**
>
> **Priority Return:** The percent of return investors will receive before profits can be split between the investors and producers. (Priority returns are often between 110 and 125 percent of investment.)
>
> Example: We had a 110 percent priority return, so our $100 investor had?to?make $110 before we could start ?splitting the additional profits.

Next, the business plan will contain information about the movie itself, including:

- Synopsis
- Cast and characters
- The people involved in the project
- An estimated budget
- Projected schedule for the entire project
- Marketing, distribution, and sales strategies

It is also good to include:

- An overview of the state of the movie industry as a whole
- Financial projections that show how well your film(s) may do
- And even more legal stuff describing some (but not all) of the risks involved

Although a lot of those sections may sound intimidating, most of them are fairly standard, and you'll likely find that with some hard work, writing this is something you or your team is capable of. And, if you find that you're not the right person to write your business plan, you can hire a lawyer or producer to put the document together for you. There are even people who do nothing but write business plans for a living.

If you do write the business plan yourself, put as much work into it as possible, and then have a lawyer review it before giving it out to potential investors. There are laws about how you can go about offering investments and securities, with many states requiring that certain wording and disclaimers be included. So let a lawyer help keep you out of any potential hot water.

After pouring days or even months into the document, know that your potential investors may never even read it. They may give it to their accountant or lawyer to review, or it may barely get skimmed at all. Regardless, the simple existence of your business plan is critical to your film being taken seriously as an investment opportunity. Once again, it's like your resume: it may not get you a job, but no one will take you seriously if you don't have one. The business plan has to be a compelling sales tool, and it has to be professional because some savvy investors will absolutely painstakingly review it (or have their accountant and/or lawyer do so).

Key Points

- Film is a business.
- Business and art are not mutually exclusive.
- You should have a business plan for your film to be taken seriously as an investment opportunity.
- When someone gives you money for your film, it is an investment, not a gift.
- You can write your own business plan.
- The business plan alone may not get your movie financed, but it is often a crucial step in the financing process.

Fuck-Up #16

"I Don't Need a Lawyer"

When and why a lawyer is needed

"He who is his own lawyer has a fool for a client."[12]
—author unknown

The Fuck-Up...

Many filmmakers try to minimize the involvement of lawyers because

1. Lawyers are expensive.
2. Lawyers can slow things down.
3. Lawyers can rain on your creative parade by telling you what you shouldn't do.

All the preceding statements are true, but that doesn't outweigh the benefits of having a good lawyer involved in your movie. Sure, lawyers can be very expensive, but not having one is a mistake that can cost you a whole lot more: it could cost you money, it could cost you your movie, and it could cost you your freedom.

How to Do It Right...

This discussion on lawyers is in the "Getting the Money" section of this book only because the financing stage is likely one of the first times in your moviemaking process you'll want to consult with a lawyer, but it will be far from the last. The need for expert legal counseling is applicable to nearly every stage of the filmmaking process. When raising money, writing contracts, structuring your company, giving out points, clearing music rights, hiring crew, and putting together countless other pieces of the filmmaking puzzle, you should be consulting some sort of legal expertise to make sure you're not doing anything that can come back to haunt you later.

There are laws regarding securities offerings that a lawyer can advise you on before going out to investors. If your deals are not drafted carefully, you can end up in very hot water. If your letters of interest are not worded in your best interest, you could inadvertently end up with something that still binds you to pay an actor regardless of whether or not he ends up in the movie. At nearly every stage of the filmmaking process, it is helpful to have a lawyer available to you—even if you are trying to minimize legal involvement to keep down those pricey billable hours.

In our lawsuit-happy society, it is difficult to discuss almost any business venture without concern about protecting yourself legally. In other words: how to cover your ass. In that spirit, I must advise you that a lot of what we discuss throughout this book can become legally tricky if not approached carefully. You don't want to get your movie, or you, sued. It can be costly and, worse yet, it could prevent your movie from being finished or even released.

This is not to say that you should not take a do-it-yourself approach when possible, but merely that when in doubt, consult a professional. If you can rework an existing contract and feel comfortable with it, that might be fine. A lot of filmmakers use cookie-cutter contracts. I've seen the same deal-memos forwarded from job to job, often with the same typos still in them for years. If you want to file your own LLC paperwork and are competent, go for it. If you can get good form contracts that fit your needs, that may cover a lot of your day-to-day legal needs. The key is to know what you can do yourself and what you should absolutely leave to a legal professional. Always be cautious and make sure your ass isn't exposed to unnecessary danger, much in the manner that I am attempting to cover mine here by advising you to do so.

When in doubt, consult an attorney. Let her protect you, and try not to get too fearful of the legal stuff yourself. Remember it is part of your lawyer's job to be paranoid and worry about everything for you. She should be worried about covering you for everything that could go wrong, so you, in turn, don't need to worry so much.

Key Points

- Lawyers are expensive, but not having one can cost you much more.
- You need someone with legal expertise to protect you and your movie.
- Making a movie can open you up to a lot of sticky legal situations if not handled properly.
- For some legal needs, a "do-it-yourself" approach can work.
- When in doubt, consult an attorney.

Pre-Production

Fuck-Up #17

"We Don't Need Much Pre-Production"

Why pre-production is so damned important

"He who fails to plan, plans to fail."[1]

—author unknown

The Fuck-Up...

It can be difficult to appreciate just how much of your life shooting a movie will take up. To give a conservative estimate, I'd say it's safest to assume it will take up 100 percent of your life. That means that during your shooting: Forget about any other jobs you may have and make sure your family is supportive and understanding because you'll be neglecting them. It will be difficult to find time to mow your lawn, do your laundry, or do just about anything else you think you should be doing—because shooting your movie is so thoroughly all-consuming. Twelve hours is commonly considered a regular day on set, and when you count in overtime, the time preparing for the next day, the time spent watching dailies, rehearsing, revising your plan, and travel time, figure you're working basically every second you aren't sleeping (and don't count on sleeping too much either).

The point is, if there is anything you can take care of before the all-consuming madness of production begins, do so. And that is why pre-production is so important.

How to Do It Right...

If there is something you can do in pre-production rather than in production, do it then. It is that simple. Out of fear that some readers may not yet appreciate the value of that statement, allow me to repeat it:

> **If there is something you can do in pre-production rather than in production, do it then!**

This advice applies to absolutely every facet of preparation that goes into making a film: finding locations, making props, having wardrobe fittings, finding that giraffe you need, figuring out your shot

50

lists, finding talent, hiring crew, designing the lighting, figuring out transportation, finding lodging, hiring a caterer, figuring out where the bathrooms are, making storyboards, walking through the schedule—EVERYTHING. Some people may be resistant to this type of thinking. Many directors do not like to be restrained to things like shot lists or storyboards, and that's fine. Nevertheless, whatever your creative style will permit to be done in pre-production, you should go ahead and do it then. Yes, the plan is going to evolve later, but you must prepare yourself with a plan that is ready to evolve.

By the time you reach production, anything you have taken care of early will leave you more available time to deal with the countless other things that are impossible to prepare for. Every second on-set is valuable and expensive, so if you can address issues in pre-production, do it then (did I mention that already?). This requires a superpower-like sense of foresight, but the more foresight your pre-production team is capable of, the better off you will surely be in production, and thus, the better off your movie will be.

A great producer has a keen sense of foresight and will be able to eliminate most potential problems well before they arise. You should take great comfort in having a very bored-looking production staff on-set. That means they did such a good job preparing in pre-production that they eliminated the potential problems before they had a chance to turn into real problems.

There is indeed a lot to do in pre-production to ensure a good production, but no one should go at it alone. Worrying about everything means you are not paying enough attention to the things that truly should demand your attention. Delegate wherever possible to keep yourself available to deal with what should not be delegated. Make sure you have good people thinking about the details they're best at and put your trust in them. Pre-production is where you will set the precedent on how your team will interact. Establish a sense of guidance, trust, support, and collaboration. Give your crew the time, inspiration, and creative vision to properly and thoroughly prepare, and your movie will benefit immensely.

Alfred Hitchcock used to remark that filming the movie was the boring part, because he had already shot it in his head.[2] If you can accomplish much of your creative and logistical work well before the camera starts rolling, you are in very good shape to see your vision come to life and to grow.

Key Points

- If there is something you can do in pre-production rather than in production, do it then!
- A great producer can foresee problems and eliminate them well before they arise.
- Rely on your pre-production team. Give them what they need to prepare, and your movie will benefit immensely.

Fuck-Up #18

"I Don't Want SAG Actors"

Why limiting your talent pool can cripple your movie

"Casting is everything. If you get the right people, they make you look good."[3]
—Todd Solondz

The Fuck-Up...

Dealing with guilds and unions can be difficult and expensive. And no guild in the entertainment industry is as powerful or expensive to deal with as the Screen Actors Guild (SAG). However, when it comes to actors, as with any job you want done well, it is safest to hire experienced professionals—and that often means using SAG actors.

How to Do It Right...

Bad acting is a trademark of bad filmmaking. Unless you are intentionally trying to make a film that will be considered bad, you are going to want to hire capable actors. Most experienced film actors belong to the Screen Actors Guild (they may also be members of the Actors' Equity union). This means in order to hire the most capable actors possible for your film, your movie will have to become signatory to the Screen Actors Guild.

> **THE LINGO**
>
> **Signatory:** A producer, film, or production company that has signed a union's or guild's collective bargaining agreement. This obligates the signatory to comply with the guild's or union's rules.

Some filmmakers take the approach of hiring only unknown actors. It is always great to discover new talent and to give new actors an opportunity. However, if you take this approach, audition carefully. As with any job, experience helps, and although many less experienced actors are remarkably talented, experienced actors do know many tricks of the trade that can greatly improve their performances and make things a lot easier on the people behind the camera. It is very expensive to discover an actor's shortcomings while shooting your movie or, worse yet, after it has been shot. With experienced actors, the odds of their being capable at their work increases exponentially.

Another approach sometimes taken to avoid hiring actors at all is what's called "real people casting." With this approach, you attempt to hire individuals who are so similar to the characters they will be playing that there will be little acting required. Although this is certainly an exciting approach to casting, I'd advise a good deal of caution when considering it. Good actors make the director, writer, and everyone else involved in a film look good at their respective jobs. Capable actors will take the script and the character to higher levels, expanding on what is on the page to make it better than perhaps you ever thought possible. Often, the best thing a director can do is cast well and let the actors make him look good. However, if you take the risk of hiring less experienced or less capable actors, you are likely to spend less time helping them make you look good and more time attempting to prevent them from making you look bad.

There are countless tricks to good acting (many of which we'll discuss later in the "Acting" section of this book), such as camera awareness, continuity awareness, knowing how to act differently in clean shots versus dirty shots, and so on. Through practice, experienced actors are likely to have mastered many of these tricks. As in any job, hiring professionals allows you to lean on their experience and expertise. And hiring amateurs can be risky and costly.

Good actors will give you many options of great usable material when it comes time to edit your film. Conversely, with inexperienced actors, when it comes time to edit, you may find yourself struggling to cut their poor acting out of your movie.

Key Points

- Bad acting is a trademark of bad filmmaking.
- The most experienced and capable actors are likely to be members of the Screen Actors Guild.
- Some films take the approach of hiring nonunion talent.
- Hiring nonunion talent increases the odds of having less capable actors.
- Good actors make everyone look good.
- Having good actors allows the director to spend more time focusing on other things.
- There are countless tricks that experienced actors are already familiar with that will enable them to do their job well.

Fuck-Up #19

"Cast the Person Who Looks the Part"

Why it is never good to cast looks over talent

"Casting is 65 percent of directing."[4]
—John Frankenheimer

The Fuck-Up...

New filmmakers often suffer from a crippling inability to change how they envision certain aspects of their film. They have an image of how specific elements should look and have trouble allowing that image to evolve, whether it's for better or worse. Perhaps this is most true in the way new filmmakers envision their characters.

During casting, someone who looks almost exactly the way you imagined the character might walk into the room, and you will want to cast that person. However, casting based on appearance over ability is a very rookie mistake and one that you will be likely to regret.

How to Do It Right...

Kurt Russell was the early frontrunner to play Han Solo in *Star Wars*. Queen Latifah's character in her film *Last Holiday* was originally written for a white male lead. Matthew McConaughey was the studio's first pick over Leonardo DiCaprio to star in *Titanic*. And O.J. Simpson was almost the title character in *Terminator* over Arnold Schwarzenegger.

The way we envision a character can change. Films are constantly evolving, and must do so in order to survive. However, what cannot change is an actor's lack of ability (for an example, see any Paris Hilton movie). If you cast someone solely because she "looks the part," then chances are you are not casting the most capable actor—the one who will truly bring something special to the role and make it even better than you could have ever imagined. You must always allow yourself to keep a somewhat open mind. Although an actor's appearance is absolutely important, it should never be the sole casting criterion.

One common first-time filmmaker approach is to make a movie that is in many ways autobiographical to the filmmaker. Thus, a lot of first movies somehow end up with leads that bear a rather striking resemblance to the filmmaker. While your life story may (or may not) be worthy of telling, casting your doppelganger is a risky approach. If the characters are based on real people who are not recognizable famous figures, do not get hung up on your mental image of how they look. Remember, you are creating another world; even the most true-to-reality story is still fiction. Like Austrian filmmaker Michael Haneke said, "Film is 24 lies per second at the service of truth."[5] Don't be afraid to lie; after all, that's the job.

Consider carefully what is most important about a particular character and let that determine what to look for in an actor. Is it a role that's about the look and will require no acting ability? If so, you might be okay casting solely for appearance. However, in most cases, the part is going to require acting ability. If you need the character to be believable, sympathetic, funny, compelling, dramatic, and/or simply well acted, you must weigh those needs in relation to the actor's appearance. Chances are, when you start thinking about such priorities, you'll realize that although a character's appearance is an absolutely critical factor, it is not the most critical.

Key Points

- Casting the person who most resembles how you imagine the character instead of casting the most capable actor is almost always a mistake.
- An actor's talent and appearance are both important.
- New filmmakers often get overly hung up on how they imagine a particular character's appearance.
- Your characters, like everything in your film, must be able to evolve and change for the benefit of the film.
- Decide what characteristics are most important for a particular role and then look for an actor who fits those priorities.

Fuck-Up #20

"We Don't Need Much Equipment"

What gear you really need

"If you ain't got no axe, you cain't cut no wood."[6]
—John Eaton

The Fuck-Up...

The day before I was to direct my first student film, a friend and I showed up in a cab to pick up the equipment that our director of photography (also called the D.P.) had ordered. We quickly realized there was vastly more than a cab's full and had no idea how we were going to transport it all. We called the D.P. in a panic, pleading "Do we really need all this?" to which he replied, "It's really not that much."

I had fallen victim to a common new filmmaker naiveté, not appreciating just how much equipment is likely to be involved even in my "little film." Although I was shocked then, many years later I came to realize my D.P. had been completely right; compared to most productions, our equipment order was, in fact, tiny. Worse yet, I had committed a bigger mistake, not making sure my crew and I were on the same page.

How to Do It Right...

What you see on-screen gives no impression of how much gear was used behind the camera. If you are new to filmmaking, there's a good chance you will be shocked at just how much equipment professionals will tell you they need to accomplish their jobs effectively. However, you hire professionals for a reason, and you must rely on their expertise.

Whenever possible, it is always better to be overprepared. Your plan will be constantly evolving, so having the proper equipment for various scenarios allows for the possibility of adaptation. Part of why studio films cost so much money is that they allow themselves to have the equipment for many scenarios. Most of the equipment present daily on a major Hollywood set may never be used, but it is there to keep options open. Of course, few of us in the independent film world can afford such luxuries, so consult with your crew to put together the right equipment to accomplish what you want and leave room for the plan to change—without breaking your budget.

Meanwhile, be aware that, if allowed to, most people will spend money. The majority of people in film do what they do because they love it and, given the resources, would love to do it on a larger scale. The art department can always have more elaborate sets, the costume department can always have more wardrobe options, the grips and electrics can always have more toys, and so on. So although you want your crew equipped and prepared, they must also be reined in at times to keep things at a level that is reasonable for the project and its limitations.

In this age of digital filmmaking, the idea of making a film with very little equipment has become increasingly popular. As technology continues to improve, it is increasingly possible to get better results while spending less money on equipment. However, many film professionals would advise a good deal of caution with this mentality. They'd argue that, aesthetically, actual celluloid film provides much more natural beauty than any digital format. So you may find yourself spending a lot more money and time in lighting and equipment to get a digital image looking good. In that manner, digital does not necessarily translate to less equipment; it will depend on your film, your crew, the quality of that equipment, and your approach to keeping things small.

As always, the most important thing is to find the plan that best suits your movie, and make sure you have the right crew and the right budget to fit that plan. If you want to use just a camera and available light, that's great, as long as your crew members are on board and won't be complaining about the lack of equipment they have to work with. If you want to have a big shoot that will allow you Hollywood looks and freedom, that's also great—assuming your budget and crew can get on board.

> **THE LINGO**
>
> **Available Light:** Any source of pre-existing light not provided by the filmmakers. This can include the sun, moon, or any pre-existing lighting at a location.

Key Points

- What happens on the screen gives little impression of how much equipment it took to accomplish it.
- Those new to filmmaking are often surprised by how much equipment is involved.
- It is always better to be overprepared than underprepared.
- Trust the expertise of your crew to tell you what they need.
- Remember that if allowed, people will generally want to have more equipment than may be necessary.
- Digital filmmaking does not necessarily mean you will need less equipment.
- Always make sure that you have a crew and budget that aligns with the way you want to approach making your movie.

Fuck-Up #21

"We Don't Need to Go on a Scout"

Why you need scouts and what to do while you're there

"The general who wins the battle makes many calculations in his temple before the battle is fought. The general who loses makes but few calculations beforehand."[7]

—Sun Tzu

The Fuck-Up…

Shooting a location you have not seen is going to go about as well as shooting a script you have not read. Scouting is one of the best tools you have to plan your shoot and to get your crew informed of that plan ahead of time. New filmmakers often underappreciate the importance of scouting, only to show up on a shoot day and discover all sorts of problems that they could have prepared for and fixed ahead of time had they only scouted properly.

How to Do It Right…

There are two main types of scouts:

- "Location scouts" involve visiting potential shooting locations to find out which ones may or may not work for your shoot.
- "Tech scouts" (also called "tech recce" or "technical reconnaissance") occur after a location is chosen. On tech scouts, necessary crew members visit the selected shooting locations to assess their needs and plan for shooting there.

Let's start our discussion with the first type, location scouts.

Location Scouts

An interesting location can change your entire vision of a scene and take it to a higher level. However, there are several factors that make a "good location":

- Does the location look the part? Locations are another character in your film, and changing locations can change the feel of a scene entirely. Think carefully about what in the location will end up on camera and whether it will accomplish the look desired.
  At the same time, try to ignore the parts of the location that will not end up on camera. Remember, you control what the audience will see, so if you can make the on-camera part of a location work, the audience never needs to know about what is off-camera.
- Does the location allow for the type of camera work you are imagining, or would you have to knock down walls to get the camera where it needs to be (which is fine, if you can in fact knock down their walls)?
- Is the location controllable? Shooting in one corner of a restaurant that is open for business is going to make your life and the life of everyone else there very unpleasant. So think carefully whether you'll be able to really control the space adequately during filming.
- Does the location provide the necessary off-set resources you'll need? You know how big your "company" is. So does the location or do nearby locations allow space for the grip and electric equipment, production offices, hair, makeup, dressing rooms, and a place for the crew to eat lunch and use the bathroom? If all of the above is going to happen in trucks and/or

trailers, is there the necessary parking nearby? Furthermore, is there available space to put all the vehicles that will bring all the stuff that comes with making a movie?

- Is the location owner comfortable with what will happen there during filming? Some new filmmakers don't want to scare the location owners or management, so they're quick to downplay the level of intrusion that the filming will cause. This is a mistake. Having location owners freaking out before your shoot is a much better option having than them freaking out on your shoot day. You should aim to overprepare your locations. The truth is, a film shoot is a huge intrusion, and location owners should know that. And if they're not okay with it, give yourself time to find location owners that are.

> **THE LINGO**
>
> **Company:** A film set is thought of as a moving "company." The entire cast, crew, vehicles, and equipment make up the company.

> **THE LINGO**
>
> **Holding:** An area near the set where necessary off-set resources are located. This is often the place where the production department has offices; talent and extras can hang out; crew meals are served; hair, makeup, and wardrobe can be staged; restrooms are accessible; batteries can be charged; and so on.
>
> Example: Our shooting location was on the street, so we rented out a nearby restaurant for holding.

- Is the location attainable? Often your locations may be decided by what you can actually get. If this is the case, make the most of whatever locations you have. A less than ideal location is far better than no location at all—even if some of the preceding factors must be compromised.

Finding the right location for a scene (or scenes) may take many location scouts. Often different people will visit the same location multiple times. It's not uncommon for a "location scout" or the "location manager" to visit first. If this person thinks a location is a contender, he then comes back with the director and other members of the creative team for further review. Keep looking at locations until you find the places that best fit the needs of your movie—or until time runs out and you are forced to choose, whichever happens first.

Tech Scouts

When you are still figuring out your locations, it is not worth dragging a bunch of your crew members around town only to show them places you may or may not end up actually using. However, after a location has been chosen, it is vital to show it to key personnel so that they can begin planning their work, make their equipment lists, and address any potential problems early.

You have departments for their specific expertise, and those individuals are the best at assessing their own needs. For an example, see season one of the *Project Greenlight* documentary, where to save money the producers didn't bring the sound mixer on a location scout. They were all shocked when it came shooting time and they realized that the elevated train they'd decided to shoot under was going to make sound recording impossible. Had they brought the sound mixer on their tech scout (as he requested), they would have had someone there thinking about sound and could have avoided this problematic location.

The production department staff need to figure out where their offices, talent holding, dining, and those always-crucial bathrooms will be located. If any of these elements are missing, they will need to determine how to compensate for them. The gaffer will look into the location's power situation: is the existing power adequate or is a generator needed? The key grip will get an understanding of the shooting and what gear and crew will be needed. The 1st A.D. (short for "assistant director") needs to get a sense of the shooting plan that is going to occur at the location, to then inform everyone else who will need to know that plan.

> **THE LINGO**
>
> **1st A.D.:** The individual in charge of creating the shooting schedule, running the set, seeing that the schedule is adhered to, arranging logistics, and directing extras.

So which people should you bring on your tech scout? If you plan on having any of the following people involved in your project, it's a good idea to take them on tech scouts if possible:

- Director
- Producer, Line Producer, Production Manager, and/or whoever will be in charge of the location for the Production Department
- Location Manager
- Director of Photography
- Production Designer
- Art Director
- 1st Assistant Director
- Gaffer
- Key Grip
- Key P.A.
- Sound Mixer

As we've learned time and again, keeping your crew informed of the plan allows them to perform their jobs efficiently and allows you to change the plan when necessary. And nothing allows people to plan better than being in the space and visualizing the work.

Sometimes during tech scouts, directors can be hesitant to really take the time to discuss every shot that will be filmed there. It's a lot of work to walk through and think about every shot, but

I assure you it is time very well spent (yes, even if the plan is still evolving and might change later). Generally, the 1st A.D. will do her best to get the director and D.P. talking about the work that is to be done at each location. The more every shot is discussed, the more thinking and planning can be accomplished ahead of time. Furthermore, walking through the shots very often causes people to begin to think about the various problems they might encounter. This, in turn, will get them thinking about solutions. And any problems you can find solutions for during your scout rather than on your very expensive shoot day is a wonderful thing. So try hard to force your creative team to fully utilize the scout to think through every single piece of work and every single shot they want to accomplish, how they want to accomplish it, and in what order they want to accomplish it.

There will likely be a lot to do on a busy scout day, and you'll need to keep things moving. So keep up the scout day momentum (remember you can discuss things while driving to your next location), but do make sure you discuss all the location's work as thoroughly as you can. Then make sure you communicate that plan to the crew members who are present as much as possible and let them ask questions. Like the Chinese proverb says, "Tell me and I'll forget; show me and I may remember; involve me and I'll understand."[8]

Key Points

- Shooting a location you have not seen is a very bad idea.
- Location scouts are when you look for shooting locations.
- Tech scouting is when the crew visits the selected location to assess their needs and plan for the shooting that is to occur there.
- Good locations have the look you want, allow for the camera work you want, are controllable, have the off-set resources you will need, and have management or owners who are comfortable with your plans for shooting there.
- It is always better to overprepare your location's management or owners for what they're in for.
- It is crucial to bring appropriate crew on tech scouts to allow them the opportunity to develop a game plan.
- Use your tech scouts both to plan as much as possible and to inform people of the plan that will need to be accomplished at each location.

Scheduling

Fuck-Up #22

"I Have to Shoot My Movie in Script Order"
Why shooting out of order shouldn't be a scary thought

"The key is not to prioritize what's on your schedule,
but to schedule your priorities."[1]
—Stephen R. Covey

The Fuck-Up...

New filmmakers often worry that shooting out of script order will make it difficult to keep track of where they are in the film's story or somehow make it harder to organize the pieces in the edit. This couldn't be further from the truth. Shooting out of order is a necessity that will only serve to make the process vastly easier.

At a Q&A, I once heard legendary director Sidney Lumet (*12 Angry Men, Dog Day Afternoon*) asked if he thought shooting a movie out of script order made it difficult for the actors. Without the slightest hesitation, Sidney's response was, "No, they're actors; they do it all the time." The answer seemed to take the interviewer by surprise, but anyone who has had experience making films knows this is the absolute norm, which is why Mr. Lumet found it such a ridiculous question to begin with.

Nearly all movies shoot out of script order, and nearly all professional actors and directors become comfortable working this way. Story is crucial, but shooting out of story order does not mean any work need suffer.

How to Do It Right...

Much of the planning that goes into making movies revolves around being as prepared as possible to change the plan when need be. Countless movies fall apart due to their schedule's inability to adapt to their circumstances. You can lose an actor because you cannot schedule around his other work/family obligations/NBA season tickets (Jack Nicholson must be scheduled around the Los Angeles Lakers' home games during the NBA season). Bad weather can kill your movie entirely if you can't come up with a plan B, as was nearly the case with the constant storms and three hurricanes that ravaged the filming of *Waterworld*. As with all of filmmaking, there are endless variables that may require you to change your plans at any time. However, with good planning, you and your schedule can be ready to adapt to the circumstances, and thus you can vastly increase the chances of success for you and your movie.

> **THE LINGO**
>
> **Line Producer:** Individual managing the day-to-day budget, crew, and logistics of a movie shoot.

Most likely, an early draft of the shooting schedule will be done by a line producer or a producer; then during pre-production, control of the schedule is given over to the 1st assistant director (also called the 1st A.D.), who will make a *more* finalized version. However, the schedule is never truly "final," and it will continue to be revised as needed throughout filming. Whether or not you ever make a movie's schedule yourself, a basic understanding of the logic that goes into a schedule is immensely helpful.

Professionals try their best to organize their schedules according to the following criteria, in order:

1. Locations
2. Actors
3. Time of Day
4. Balance of the Workload
5. Story

Let's examine why step by step.

Step 1: Locations

You would not plan a trip from London to Paris with stops in Antarctica and West Virginia. Simple geography makes such a route illogical, and you should use the same mentality when it comes to scheduling. It does not make sense to leave and return to a location more than is necessary. Even if the same location is used for only the first and last scenes of your movie, you should aim to group those scenes together in your shooting schedule. There are only so many hours in the day and so many days in your shoot. You want to use that precious time shooting rather than traveling, setting up, and breaking down the same locations again and again.

You can group scenes in your schedule to more efficiently shoot-out a location, actor, prop, vehicle, helicopter, difficult actor, or anything at all that will save you time and money by not spreading it out over more time than is necessary. Always aim to shoot-out a location after you are there so you need never come back to it.

Next, there is the question of interior versus exterior locations. Any experienced professional will encourage you to group all your exteriors as early in the schedule as possible. The philosophy here is that, like all good planning, this is preparation for adaptation. If you schedule exteriors early on and it rains, you can pull an interior scene from later in your schedule and shoot it earlier while waiting for the bad weather to pass. (If possible, on your exterior days, attempt to have cover sets already planned.) However, if you saved your exteriors for the end of the shoot and it rains, at that point you won't have any interior scenes left to film. Then you are stuck with a very expensive day in which you will likely not get much of anything you really need shot.

> **THE LINGO**
>
> **Shoot-Out:** Grouping together the work that requires a particular location, actor, or other element to complete the work that requires that element accomplished more efficiently in the schedule.
>
> Example: "We grouped together all the gorilla's scenes to shoot it out first."

> **THE LINGO**
>
> **Cover Set:** An interior set that is a backup should the weather make the exterior work scheduled for the day impossible.
>
> Example: "If it rains the day we're shooting the park scene, we'll go to our cover set and shoot in a gymnasium instead."

Step 2: Actors

You must determine when your actors are available. If you do not have their time exclusively, find out if you need to schedule around their TV show, Broadway show, waitressing job, etc. Also, do not be surprised if their availability changes. You are always planning and always ready to adapt if forced, and actors (especially amateur ones) are notorious for changing their schedules.

Scheduling actors does not just mean scheduling them on days they're available; it also means grouping to shoot-out particular actors like you did for locations. Let's say an actor is going to work three days total; it makes sense to group those days together rather than a day at the beginning of your schedule, one in the middle, and another at the end. This will save you both money and actor frustration.

The Screen Actor's Guild (SAG, the film actors' union) will likely require weekly rates rather than daily rates be paid to actors who work multiple days per week (rates and rules vary depending on the budget of your film; check out www.sagindie.org/resources/contracts/ to find out which agreement applies to your movie). SAG may require you to pay actors their weekly rate and daily per diems even if you use them only on Monday and Friday. SAG's theory is that because of the days you have the actors booked, it is unlikely they could schedule other work on the in-between days. Thus, since you might be costing the actors other work, you have to pay them for that time.

> **THE LINGO**
>
> **Per Diem:** A contractually agreed-upon sum of money paid daily to help cover an actor's daily expenses (such as food and travel).
>
> Example: "The star's per diem is more than many of us get paid for a whole movie."

Flying actors back and forth, paying off-day per diems, and just inconveniencing them are all great reasons to shoot-out actors in the most condensed manner possible. If some actors are pricier or have more scheduling conflicts, group them first. Other actors may get stuck with spread-out schedules, but, as with all these elements, you need to figure out your priorities and let the schedule reflect them.

Step 3: Time of Day

Certain scenes will likely need to be shot at certain times of day. Your ability to do so may be restricted by your need for sunlight, night, or a location's availability (many businesses will let you shoot only at hours that don't interfere with their regular business).

You must also think about your cast and crew's sleep schedules, or what in the industry is called "turnaround." If you work people all day Tuesday, all night Wednesday, and then go back to a daytime schedule Thursday, their sleep schedule will be very messed up. If you mess up people's sleep, there is a good chance you will not be getting the best out of your exhausted (and probably very angry) cast and crew. Do your best to group together all the work that will require a similar time of day. It is generally easiest to start with daylight hours and then slide the schedule to progressively later work as the shoot goes on.

> **THE LINGO**
>
> **Turnaround:** The amount of time between ending one day's work and beginning the next day's work.
>
> Example: "If we finish at 8 p.m. tonight and start at 8 a.m. tomorrow, the crew will get a 12-hour turn around."

To help make scheduling easier, you may want to consider shooting some scenes day-for-night or conversely night-for-day.

Often you will truly need night-for-night and day-for-day. This depends on the location and your ability to control it. If you are shooting outdoors and need true night, it may not be very easy to block out the sun. However, if you're shooting in a windowless room, there really isn't much visual reference for the time of day and you can shoot whenever without worry. Examine your scenes and consult with your director of photography (D.P.) about which scenes can be shot when for scheduling purposes.

THE LINGO

Day-for-Night: Making a scene look like nighttime while shooting it in the day.

Night-for-Day: Making a scene look like daytime while shooting it at night.

Example: "If we block the light from all the windows, we can shoot the scene day-for-night."

Step 4: Balance of the Workload

The length of your script divided by the number of days in your schedule will determine the average page count you will need to shoot per day. If you have a 100-page script and a 20-day shoot, then you need to average 5 pages per day. Realistically, daily page counts can average anywhere from a low of ½ page to an extreme high of 13 pages per day (but hopefully somewhere in between). It is important to try to balance your workload evenly to make every day accomplishable. So as you work on your schedule, do your best to keep the daily page counts near your "average page per day" number to spread the work evenly.

The number of pages, however, is not always a clear reflection of the amount of work implied. Screenwriter Robert Towne (*Chinatown, The Firm*) found this out when writing *Mission Impossible II* for director John Woo. Mr. Woo would turn a simple line in the script like "a car chase ensues" into a complex 15-minute action sequence, which likely took weeks to shoot. For Mr. Woo, shooting a small fraction of a page per day (if those pages were an action scene) was fine because he had the schedule and budget to make that possible. Likewise, you must determine what average workload your schedule and budget allow.

Some low-budget films are known for shooting upwards of 8–12 pages per day (they probably do not involve John Woo–like car chases). Do your best to balance not just the number of pages, but also the work reflected within those scenes. If one day seems overloaded, slide some of that material to a lighter day. This will ensure that all your days are more equally accomplishable.

Step 5: Story

Deciding whether or not to attempt emotionally draining scenes first, or to allow your actors time to learn their characters, can greatly influence their performances. Waiting until actors know each other before attempting a love scene can affect on-screen chemistry. In many instances, knowing how one scene plays out can influence how you would approach another scene. Some directors simply like to get the more difficult work out of the way early, so they can feel more relaxed later. Or there's Michael Bay (*Transformers, Pearl Harbor*), who is known for getting the dialogue-driven material over with early and quickly in his schedules so that he can spend more time concentrating on action sequences.

In contrast, the film *A Beautiful Mind* was shot entirely in script order to help Russell Crowe develop his character chronologically. This is a wonderful luxury that most films simply cannot afford. Nevertheless, while Russell Crowe got an Oscar nomination for that remarkable performance, Sidney Lumet, who never even thought about shooting in script order, directed 17 actors to Oscar nominations. Either approach may be valid, but there is no doubt that Mr. Lumet's approach saves time and money. And saving time and money is what is likely to make completing your film possible.

Key Points

- Shooting in script order is often impossible and nearly always impractical.
- Good planning helps you be prepared to change the plan.
- The responsibility for making and maintaining the shooting schedule belongs primarily to the 1st assistant director and line producer.
- First, try to group work based on location, then talent, and then time of day. Next, try to balance your workload, and lastly, schedule based on story needs and director's preference.
- Put exteriors as early in the schedule as possible.
- Try not to confuse people's sleep cycles more than is absolutely necessary.
- Try to balance the workload evenly between your days.
- A director must try to predict how scheduling will influence actors' performances.
- The schedule will change.

Fuck-Up #23

"I Don't Need a Stripboard Schedule"
Why you'll never know how you lived without a stripboard after you've had one

"How many times do I have to tell you? The right tool for the right job!"[2]
—Scotty, *Star Trek V: The Final Frontier*

The Fuck-Up...

There are countless ways to make a schedule, and many would-be filmmakers have their own systems—nearly all of which fall short of how the pros do it. No system is as thought out and effective a way to make and organize a schedule as the professional standard stripboard schedule.

How to Do It Right...

A professional shooting schedule is done in what is called a "stripboard." In ye olden pre-computer days of filmmaking, this was actually a long accordion-shaped object full of individual strips of paper. Each strip represented a particular scene and had information on it about that scene, such as the location, scene number, time of day, whether it was interior or exterior, the characters in that scene, its page length, and so on. The strips could be slid in and out of the accordion and moved around as the schedule was reworked.

Today the schedule is done on a computer, and virtual strips are shifted around an electronic stripboard (a sample stripboard you can use to get started is available online at filmmakerfups.com. If you can afford it, professional scheduling software is also available and very helpful). Stripboards are customizable. Let's take a look at a sample. Figure 23.1 shows two days of a movie's shooting schedule.

Sheet #: 2 1pg	Scene: 2	EXT	Bar Guy walks out of bar.	Day	1
Sheet #: 3 1pg	Scene: 3	EXT	Street Guy walks down street and meets Other Guy.	Night	1, 3
End of Day 1 - Friday, February 17, 2015.			**Pg total: 2**		
Sheet #: 1 1pg	Scene: 1	INT	Bar Guy walks in to bar.	Day	1, 2
Sheet #: 4 1pg	Scene: 4	INT	Room Guy and Other Guy go into room.	Night	1, 3
End of Day 2 - Saturday, February 18, 2015.			**Pg total: 2**		

Figure 23.1 *Sample stripboard. (For color image please see page 1 of the insert.)*

The first thing you may notice is that the strips are color coded. The meanings of the colors are not always standardized from movie to movie, and you can utilize your own color system. Just be sure to make your system consistent throughout your own schedule to avoid confusion. For the purpose of this example, here's what the colors mean:

- Yellow = Exterior Day
- Green = Exterior Night
- Red = Interior Day
- Blue = Interior Night

The color system is an important aid in grouping scenes because it helps you quickly identify what scenes are day or night as well as interior or exterior. As you know, it is helpful to schedule all your exteriors as early in your shoot as possible. It also does not make sense to schedule a day of exterior work sequenced: a day scene, then a night scene, and then another day scene. Thus, the colors give you a quick and easy reference to help you organize and group scenes logically.

Understandably, those new to looking at stripboards often think that the black sections represent a summary of the information below it, but be aware that the reverse is true: it's a summary of what came *before* it. Notice that in our sample stripboard, we intend to shoot two scenes each day. Scenes two and three are scheduled for day 1, and scenes one and four are scheduled for day 2. Each of these individual scenes is one page long, and we hope to shoot two pages' worth of work on both days, so it appears our workload is well balanced.

Stripboards are customizable so that you can include whatever information is helpful to you and your schedule. Some of the more standard information included on strips includes:

Locations

In our example, the locations are "Bar," "Street," and "Room," respectively. You will pull this information from the scene headings (also called "slug lines") in your script.

> **THE LINGO**
>
> **Scene Headings (aka Slug Lines):** In a script, the line at the beginning of a scene that sets up that scene. Includes exterior or interior, the location, and time of day.
>
> Example: "Int. The Psycho's Basement—Night"

Scene Numbers

A proper shooting script has all the scenes numbered. Once the script is "locked," the scene numbers must not change—even if the script does.

> **THE LINGO**
>
> **Locked Script:** A script with all the scene numbers assigned.

A lot of things will be planned based on these scene numbers. Actors will learn their lines based on the knowledge that you are shooting scene #*x* tomorrow. Props, wardrobe, makeup, grip, electric, and camera departments are all going to generate reports of what they need on what days based on these numbers. So after a script is locked, added scenes will be given a letter. If you add a scene between scene 1 and scene 2, it will be called scene 1A. Likewise, if you delete scene 1, it will stay in the schedule as "Scene 1 Omitted," which will prevent any confusion as to missing numbers. No matter what happens after a scene is assigned a number in a locked script, it keeps that number; otherwise, terrible confusion is sure to ensue.

Sheet Numbers

The stripboards might also mention what number "breakdown sheet" corresponds to a scene.

Breakdown sheets provide much more information than could possibly fit into your stripboard. On the breakdown sheet will be a plethora of information including, but not limited to: cast, background actors, stunts, vehicles, props, cameras, special effects, ward-robe, makeup, hair, animals, music, sound, art department, set dressing, greenery, special equipment, security, additional labor, visual effects, mechanical effects, and any "special notes" (a sample breakdown sheet is available to use at filmmakerfups.com).

> **THE LINGO**
>
> **Breakdown Sheet:** A sheet that corresponds to a particular scene and details the needs for shooting that scene.

Every department should have its own breakdowns describing when it will need what items and what labor. Thus, these reference numbers, like scene numbers, quickly become very important reference tools and should not change.

Talent

Those numbers on the far right of the strip represent characters in the movie. Every character is assigned a number. In this example the characters are numbered:

1. Guy
2. Girl
3. Other Guy

You may feel it is demeaning assigning numbers to people, but I assure you it is not. Actors are used to it. This is the way scheduling has traditionally been done for a long time and is simply a logical system to quickly realize what characters you need on what days.

End-of-Day Slugs

End-of-day slugs are the solid black lines marking the end of a day's work (it is referred to as a "day's work" whether the work is actually done during the day or night). Above the slug is the place where you list the scenes you hope to shoot that day.

Solid slugs are also given for days off so that every day on the calendar is accounted for. This makes it easy not only to rework scenes within a given day, but also to reshift entire days or even weeks on the schedule if need be.

Key Points

- A stripboard is the best tool for scheduling your movie.
- Stripboards contain a plethora of helpful information.
- Every strip represents a scene and gives information on that scene, such as its location, scene number, sheet number, necessary talent, interior or exterior, and time of day.
- After a script is locked, the scene numbers should never change.
- Stripboards will make it easier to rearrange your schedule.

Budgeting

Fuck-Up #24

"Movies Cost ____ Dollars"

Why it may be more or less expensive than you think

"You'd be surprised how much it costs to look this cheap."[1]
—Dolly Parton

The Fuck-Up...

The common conception that "movies cost millions of dollars" is quite frequently true. Movies can also cost hundreds of millions of dollars, hundreds of thousands of dollars, thousands of dollars, and in some (very rare) cases, just a few dollars. Although it's true that movies *can* cost all these amounts, where people go wrong is in assuming that movies *have* to cost any of these amounts.

How to Do It Right...

"Low budget" is another one of those fantastically vague terms (much like the term "producer") that can mean very different things depending on whom you're talking to. The simple truth is that while to many of us, spending $40,000 is a massive sum of money, a studio considers $40,000,000 to be "low budget." Furthermore, many filmmakers love referring to their films as "low budget," regardless of the price tag. Deborah Kaplan complained about the "low budget" she had to make *Josie and the Pussycats*: $22,000,000.

Michael Bay produces what he refers to as "low budget" horror films at around $12,000,000 each. And the reality is, they're right. Compared to most studio films, these movies are bargains. At the same time, hits like *El Mariachi* ($8,000), *The Blair Witch Project* ($60,000), and *Paranormal Activity* ($6,000) are also icons of "low budget" filmmaking.

> **THE LINGO**
>
> **Low Budget:** A vague term whose meaning will completely vary depending on who's using it.
>
> Example: "Our low budget movie had somewhere between $1 and $50,000,000."

Although terminology can be vague (if not completely meaningless), dollar amounts are very real things. If you don't think you can scrape together $40,000,000 from under your couch cushions, fear not; you can still make a movie.

The approach to this problem is simple: start with the budget. As we discussed in *Fuck-Up #2: "I Just Want to Make a Movie,"* if you can raise $100, then set out to make a movie with a $100 budget. If you can raise $200,000,000, then set out to make a $200,000,000 movie. As always, be ambitious and aim to do as much as you can with the resources you have. We already know that through exploiting things such as tax incentives (discussed in *Fuck-Up #12: "I Don't Care about Tax Incentives"*), you may not need to raise the entirety of your budget at all. Furthermore, as you fundraise, you may find out you can raise more money than you thought possible (as discussed in *Fuck-Up #6: "I'll Never Get the Money"*). Conversely, you may also find yourself coming up short and needing to adjust your plans.

Over the next several *Fuck-Ups*, we'll discuss tips for budgeting your movie. While making your budget, remember the important question is not "Can I make a 'low budget' movie?" but rather "What can my budget be?" With that in mind, let's discuss budgeting further, which leads us to our next *Fuck-Ups*…

Key Points

- Movies come in all budget sizes.
- "Low budget" is a vaguely defined term.
- Start with an attainable budget goal before deciding on what movie to make.

Fuck-Up #25

"You Have to Buy Stuff"

Why filmmaking is a rental business

"Everything is temporary. Everything is bound to end."[2]

—Keren Ann

The Fuck-Up...

People outside the film world often ask those in it questions such as "So you own all this equipment?" or "All these people work for you?" Most people work full-time jobs, report to the same location, and perform mostly the same tasks year round. Likewise, most companies own the equipment they need for their day-to-day business needs. So it can be a baffling concept to many that most of the labor and equipment involved in moviemaking is by nature acquired only temporarily.

How to Do It Right...

In 1888, Thomas A. Edison and his assistant W.K.L Dickson (who some people think did most of the inventing) set out to create some of the first movie cameras, or what Edison described as "an instrument which does for the eye what the phonograph does for the ear, which is the recording and reproduction of things in motion."[3] Edison and Dickson knew they needed labor to help make these early films, but they didn't want to employ full-time help when they needed only a few days of work. So they hired mostly off-duty sailors who were happy to make a little extra money while they were in port for a short time. This sense of needing temporary labor to make movies has changed little throughout the history of filmmaking. (On an interesting side note, those sailors are why so much film terminology derives from sailing terms. The gaffs are the poles on a ship, and the gaffer is the head sailor in charge of rigging them. Today, the gaffer rigs the lights on set. The "best boy" on a ship was either the gaffer or the captain's favorite crew member and thus served as his right-hand man; today the "best boy" is still the gaffer's right-hand man or woman).

Today, films are still crewed by temporary labor, using temporarily rented equipment. Individuals who make their livings on film crews go from job to job and employer to employer. This temporary-use nature of filmmaking greatly affects the budgeting process. When you're figuring out your budget, the question you need to answer is rarely "How much will this cost me to buy" but rather "How much will it cost me to rent and how long will I have to rent it?" Often it makes sense to start with that second question first. Knowing how many days, weeks, or months you need something can in large part determine what (if anything) you can afford to pay for it.

Day Out of Days

Just as every film is unique, every day making a film has its own unique and thus temporary needs. In this manner, filmmaking lends itself to a rental model—and not just movie to movie but often day to day. Filmmakers rent gear, actors' and crew members' time, locations, and so on, all based on what they will need any given day.

The "Day Out of Days" is a document that shows on what days you will require what items. "Day Out of Days" reports can be generated for anything: cast, vehicles, locations, stunt people, props, and so on. This tool comes in handy in budgeting in order to figure out how many days each expense will be needed.

Figure 25.1 shows a sample "Day Out of Days Report for Cast Members." This one corresponds to the sample stripboard used earlier in our discussion on scheduling.

Date	17-Feb	18-Feb							
Day of Wk	**Fri**	**Sat**	**Travel**	**Work**	**Hold**	**Holiday**	**Start**	**Finish**	**TOTAL**
Shooting Day	1	2							
1. Guy	SW	WF	1	2	1	0	17-Feb	18-Feb	4
2. Girl		SWF	1	1	0	0	18-Feb	18-Feb	2
3. Other Guy	SW	WF	1	2	1	0	17-Feb	18-Feb	4

Figure 25.1 *Sample "Day Out of Days Report for Cast Members."*

Characters are listed by their appropriate number: 1. Guy, 2. Girl, 3. Other Guy. Then the days are listed to the right of their names. A day will be blank if that cast member is not needed that day. However, if cast members are needed that day, the report will say either:

- **SW (Start Work):** On their first working day
- **W (Work):** On a work day that is neither their first nor last
- **WF (Work Finish):** On their last day of work
- **SWF (Start Work Finish):** Meaning they're needed only one day and thus that is both their first and last day.

The Day Out of Days report should also mention any hold, drop-off, pick-up, holidays, or travel days because they will also need to be scheduled and budgeted for.

"Hold" days are the days when an actor is not required to do any filming but is still getting paid. Depending on what guild agreement you are using, there will be days that you are required to pay actors even though they are not working. You will continue to have to pay certain hold days until those actors' work on the movie is finished.

"Drop-off" and "pick-up" days are exactly what you probably already guessed. Let's say your actor is traveling from out of town. If you do not reserve that travel time, believe it or not, that actor might not be available to get on the plane and travel that day; therefore, that time needs to be budgeted and scheduled. If you need crew or equipment to be dropped off several days after filming is completed or picked up day(s) before, that time must also be budgeted. However, for most rentals, drop-off and pick-up days will not be charged (as long as you have the items back by the rental house's specified time).

When you know how many days you will need something or someone, you can begin to multiply that amount of time by the cost of each item or individual. Costs can vary greatly, which leads us to our next *Fuck-Up*.

Key Points

- Film is a rental business.
- Most of the equipment and people involved in making movies are needed, and thus paid for, only temporarily.
- "Day Out of Days" reports list on what days you will need the items necessary to make your movie.
- Hold days, pick-up days, and drop-off days often must also be budgeted for.
- After knowing when you will need something, you can begin to calculate how much it'll cost.

Fuck-Up #26

"The Rates Are the Rates"

Why no cost is fixed

"Listen to the mustn'ts, child. Listen to the don'ts.
Listen to the shouldn'ts, the impossibles, the won'ts.
Listen to the never haves, then listen close to me...
Anything can happen, child. Anything can be."[4]
—Shel Silverstein

The Fuck-Up...

After you have a sense of how many days you'll need the various people and equipment necessary to take to make your movie, the next step is finding out what they cost per day, week, or month. You'll call rental houses, crew members, and colleagues with prior budgeting experience to get prices. And while this is very valuable research, the mistake new filmmakers make is in believing these numbers simply "are what they are."

How to Do It Right...

Crew

When budgeting crew, very often if you look hard enough, you can find people willing to work the various crew jobs at almost any rate. Many individuals are either hungry to get into film or hungry to get *further* into film and thus will work for rates proportional to their experience level—or lack thereof. This is particularly true if you're making a movie in an area with a thriving filmmaking community with plenty of aspiring filmmakers and crew but not enough opportunities for them to explore their crafts.

As with many things in life, when it comes to crew, you often get what you pay for. A more experienced crew is less likely to be willing to work for low rates. Those newer to film are often willing to work for less money because they are likely doing it out of passion for filmmaking and the opportunity to break into the industry (they certainly aren't doing it for the money), but their inexperience often shows in the work and thus makes your life more difficult.

In many cases, less seasoned crews more than make up for lack of experience with their devotion and willingness to work. Some of the best people who worked the hardest and were the most dedicated on my sets were not getting paid at all. And this is a statement you hear from filmmaker after filmmaker; it is often those who get paid the least that are willing to give the most. Weigh this fact against your budget constraints and the realization that with a less experienced crew you may spend a good amount of time doing "on-the-job training."

Entire films have been made in which the crew was not paid at all. If that is, in fact, your plan, keep in mind that means the crew had better really believe in your project. It's going to take a lot of passion to make someone else's movie for no financial compensation. Also, don't be surprised when professionals turn down your offer to work for free no matter how great "the script, project, people, or experience." Those more seasoned have heard these lines before and aren't likely to be excited by promises of the experience without compensation. You should respect that being on the crew is a job and everyone has to make a living. Volunteering their services may not be economically possible for those who need to work to pay their rent or feed their families.

Perhaps the metaphorical opposite of the free crew is the union crew. Unions have regulations that determine rates, overtime, pension and health payments, and a litany of other costs. Depending on the size, scope, and location of your movie, you may or may not decide to make your movie with any or all of your crew being union members. Unions (sometimes called guilds) exist for grips, electricians, teamsters, hair, makeup, wardrobe, assistant directors, production coordinators, composers, editors, and pretty much every other job involved in the making of movies. Unions have set and published rates. However, the mistake here is thinking that just because they're "union rates" they are not negotiable. Unions want their people working, and this is especially true in times of economic slowdown when their members may be working less frequently. Unions will very often negotiate their rates, especially if they have a lot of nonworking union members and there's a choice between their people working or the job going to nonunion labor. Union power and control vary by territory and budget level, so it's important to figure out if the local unions will be interested in a movie of your size shooting in the area. This might mean consulting other producers or, if all else fails, calling the unions and asking them if they'd want their people working on your film, and if so, what types of rates you can get.

In between the extremes of free labor and union labor, you will find "nonunion professionals." These are the many working professionals who are professionally experienced but do not belong to any union. Thus, they will need to negotiate their rates as individuals. This can be a good compromise if you'd like a fairly experienced crew but simply cannot afford union rates. The truth is, I have worked with both union and nonunion crews, and have had remarkably good and bad experiences with both. It is often more a question of the individuals, their experience, professionalism, and fit for your movie that makes the difference rather than their union status.

It's important to decide what type of crew fits your project, the way you want to make your movie, the people you want to make it with, and your budget. And then make sure your crew is on board with that plan from the outset.

Equipment

Much of the preceding discussion about the varying nature of what crews should cost can be applied to equipment. Just because one rental house gives you a particular quote for a camera, sound gear, lighting equipment, and so on does not mean that the "rate is the rate." You have to comparison shop, negotiate, and hustle to get the best rates possible for the best equipment possible.

Just like unions want their people working, rental houses want their equipment working. Gear doesn't earn them any money sitting on the shelf. So negotiate with rental houses as much as you can. Get quotes from multiple houses and ask if they can beat each other's quotes. Also, be open to customizing your order to some degree. You may know exactly what you want, but ask the rental house if there's something similar you can get a significantly better deal on. Also, talk to your crew members about what compromises they can make on their equipment needs. Finding ways to compromise what gear you need can greatly reduce rental costs. Of course, you should always do this within reason; not having the gear you need to make your movie can be even more expensive than rental costs.

If negotiating doesn't get you far enough, pleading poverty is an age-old part of indie filmmaking. Tell the rental house how much you'd love to pay full price if only you could, but you simply can't. Then ask if they can still help you out. A lot of places will give new filmmakers huge discounts (and sometimes even free gear entirely). Furthermore, if you or anyone on your crew can throw the rental house other business, that can help as well. Offer to pay full price for the commercial/music video/industrial film you're doing on the side in exchange for a good discount on stuff for your movie.

And if the rental houses still aren't giving you the types of deals you need, look for private vendors. A lot of D.P.s and assistant camera (A.C.) people own cameras, many gaffers own trucks full of lighting equipment, and plenty of sound guys and gals have their own gear. Often bypassing the rental house entirely and going right to "owner/operators" can get you much better deals because these individuals don't carry the huge overhead expenses of the big rental houses.

After you've hustled, negotiated, and hustled some more, you may get to a point where the rates just do not get any lower. The reality is that filmmaking is a business, and everyone has to make a living. At some point, you may have to accept that the best rate possible may not be what you had hoped for—but remember, accept that only after trying to negotiate because "the rate" is never simply "the rate."

Key Points

- What anything "costs" varies depending on whom you ask.
- Crew members are available at all price ranges.
- Experience will vary with price.
- More experienced crew members are likely to be more expensive.
- Less experienced crew members are likely to prove more devoted to a project.
- Some crew will work for free given the right motivation and dedication.

- You should respect when something is someone's livelihood and he or she simply cannot lower his or her rate further.
- Union rates can be negotiated.
- Equipment rates can be negotiated.
- Comparison shop when pricing out equipment rentals or purchases.
- Private equipment owners may provide better deals than rental houses.
- At some point, try as you might, you may not be able to negotiate the rate any lower.

Fuck-Up #27

"People Don't Work on Credit"

The reality of deferred costs and points

> "Everything is negotiable."
> —author unknown

The Fuck-Up...

New filmmakers often don't realize that one of the greatest tools of negotiation may not be what you agree to pay now, but what you agree to pay later.

How to Do It Right...

In the world of filmmaking, there are two popular types of IOUs used to help reduce upfront payment by offering money that may be paid later—if the conditions are right.

Deferments

"Deferring" a cost simply means agreeing to pay it later, should you be able to. Unlike traditional "debt," deferments do not involve collateral and thus lack a guarantee that they ever get paid. Some producers have given deferments a bad reputation by promising deferments they have no intention of ever paying. If crew members have had such experiences in which deferred money never came in, they may be understandably hesitant to risk a repeat. Nevertheless, there are still crews and actors willing to take deferments out of the hope and trust that the payment will eventually come through. To make deferments more enticing, you can also consider offering interest.

The rules of how you can offer deferments are not carved in stone; your offer simply depends on the situation and your negotiating abilities. You can negotiate part or, in some cases, entire salaries or costs into deferments. You can attempt to defer payments until your next investor's check shows up or until your tax credit comes in. Some pay can even be deferred until the movie actually starts selling. This arrangement can be useful for attracting actors, crew, and so on when you do not have enough money to pay them as much as they would like. Some actors may take a deferment for all or (more likely) part of their pay. You can offer X dollars in upfront pay, with a deferment of Y more dollars hopefully to be paid later.

This payment approach may sound wonderful and many independent producers can quickly get deferment happy, but there are a few crucial things to keep in mind before getting carried away on the deferment train. First and foremost, you still owe the money. At whatever point income starts flowing in, individuals with deferments have a legal right to claim their cash. Depending on how the contracts read, they may be first in line before you, your investors, even your distributors. Some distributors will not take on a film if it has too many deferments because it will hinder their ability to collect income from it. Furthermore, asking for too many deferments may make you look untrustworthy to your cast and crew, and can risk insulting the people working on your film. Whether you're hiring an actor, technician, crew person, or anyone who provides a good or service that plays a part in the filmmaking process, you should always respect that as someone's job and livelihood. Asking someone to do what she does for a living purely on good faith may leave that person in a difficult financial position. Thus, the assumption that she should do it for free with the hope of pay later may not go over very well.

Deferments can make a project less appealing to investors because most deferments will have to be paid before they start getting back any of their money. It can be difficult to explain to investors why money is coming in but not going into their wallets. With this notion in mind, there is another type of incentive you can offer that will not come out of the investors' pockets: points.

Points

Points are a percentage of a film's profits. Thus, there must be profits for the points to be worth anything. Points will not be paid out until all your deferments have been paid and your investors have been completely paid back, generally with a 10 to 25 percent bonus on top (this is the investors' "priority return," which we discussed in *Fuck-Up #15: "I Don't Need a Business Plan."* After that, profits are generally split 50 percent to the investors (called "the investors' share") and 50 percent to the producers (the producers' share). Points are taken solely as a percent of the producer's share so that the investors' portion of the profits is protected. Thus investors may prefer you give out more points than deferments since it doesn't cut into their piece of the pie.

Points, like deferments, can be offered in lieu of upfront payment. But what can make points more appealing than deferments (even though they get paid later) is that they work on a percentage. A deferred payment of $100 will only ever be worth $100 (plus any interest offered). However, because points are based on a percentage of a film's profit, they are limited only by how much money the movie makes. Some actors will even work for "minimum" salaries (the lowest amount of money the union will allow them to be paid) and take all their money in points because they are that optimistic that a film is going to be wildly profitable. Tom Cruise took this exact approach with the *Mission Impossible* movies, in which he received a minimum salary while working on the movies in exchange for huge points later. That choice helped make Mr. Cruise a reported $90 million on the first *Mission Impossible* movie alone.[5]

When a person takes points in lieu of at least partial salary, it is a sign of faith in the movie and its chances of being profitable. It also provides that person a very real financial incentive to want to see the film succeed. Some indie producers give their entire crew some small number of points (even if it's a fraction of one point) so they are incentivized to work hard to make the movie a success.

If an actor, crew member, or vendor is willing to take a deferred payment or points in lieu of upfront payment, this can greatly aid you in reducing upfront costs. Just be aware of the amount of deferments and points you are racking up, what paying them back will mean, and what percent of the producers' profits you've given away. After all, should the movie be a hit, you want to give yourself a chance to reap the financial rewards as well.

Key Points

- Deferments and points can be offered in lieu of some guaranteed payments.
- Deferring a cost means agreeing to pay it later, should you be able to.
- Many crew members will be hesitant to take deferred pay.
- Points are a percentage of the producers' share of a film's profits.
- Having points provides an incentive to want to see the film be successful.
- Investors would likely prefer that producers give out points rather than deferments.
- Deferments are agreed-upon fixed sums; points are percentages contingent on a film's profits.
- Be wary of giving out too many deferments or points.

Fuck-Up #28

"My Budget Fits My Vision"

Understanding the delicate balance between your budget and vision

"It's clearly a budget. It's got a lot of numbers in it."[6]
—George W. Bush

The Fuck-Up...

New filmmakers know that the script is the basis for the budget and schedule. What they often fail to appreciate is that all three (budget, script, and schedule) must actually affect one another. Your script, budget, and schedule must participate in a dance together. Taking turns who leads and who follows is the key to the beautiful dance that is your movie.

How to Do It Right...

As you gain a sense of:

- What and who you need to make your movie
- How long you need them
- What they will cost for that period of time

you'll be putting that information into a budget that works for your movie.

A sample budget that you can use to get started is available online at filmmakerfups.com (for larger productions, I suggest using professional budgeting software). It'll give you an idea of the numerous items you might want to budget for in your movie. Look at this budget carefully, consider all the lines, and figure out if there's even an off chance you should budget for each item listed.

Budgeting, much like screenwriting and editing, will take many drafts. It's okay to make your ideal budget first. Put in everything you would love to have in a perfect world. And put in the costs at the best number you've been able to get so far (although you'll likely keep negotiating as your budgeting process continues). At times, or when in doubt, round up some numbers to leave yourself good padding—better to have budgeted too much for something than not enough.

Next, start to determine what you can shift around to make things work, while always weighing your priorities carefully. If your film has a lot of locations, you probably should give whoever is finding those locations more time and money. If you're making a costume-heavy period piece, make sure your costume department gets a little more weight to its budget line. If the director likes a lot of rehearsal, this must be budgeted accordingly. Conversely, if you have few locations, not much wardrobe to create, or do not believe in rehearsal, then perhaps those are areas where you can save money.

Some new filmmakers try to get their hands on another movie's budget because they think as long as the bottom line is similar, they can use it for their own purposes. This is a classic rookie mistake. Every movie is unique, as are its script, schedule, and demands. Getting another movie's budget can be a great resource to help you research some numbers, but it will never truly be an accurate fit for any film aside from the one for which it was created.

After you've made a draft of the budget customized to your particular film and its priorities, start taking an axe to items you don't really need. Trim numbers for things you can do on the cheap or call in favors for. If there is an area you feel even somewhat comfortable cutting, you will probably need to cut there. Cut more and more heartlessly until your budget approaches a comfortable number. If there is an area you know, without a doubt, you are not comfortable trimming, leave it alone. Always be ready to choose your battles because there will be more fights to come. Remember, it's all about priorities. Knowing what to keep is as important as knowing what to cut.

Meanwhile, throughout the budgeting process, keep one eye on your budget and the other on your script and schedule because all three of these documents need to work together. Are there things you can rearrange in your schedule so you'll need an expensive piece of equipment or an expensive actor fewer days? Do you have one actor or crew member with a really high day rate? Well, if you can group that person's work together, maybe he will give you a better deal on a weekly rate than several scattered days. How about expensive equipment that's needed on scattered days throughout the schedule? On my first movie, we couldn't afford to rent the big lights necessary for night exterior shoots for the whole shoot. So we rearranged all our night exteriors into one long weekend and paid only for a short-term rental.

And if you can't do enough with your budget and schedule to make things work, take a very hard look at what's costing the most money in your script. Are there parts of the movie you can get more creative with and change to save money? As we've seen throughout the filmmaking process, limitations can spawn great creativity, so you may need to look at your budget to determine what has to change in the script. Revisit *Fuck-Up #3: "The Script Is Done,"* to re-examine some ideas on how to make your script less expensive to shoot. As we know, these documents will constantly be evolving, so always keep on your creative thinking cap to make your script, your budget, your schedule, and ultimately your movie work.

Key Points

- The budget, script, and schedule will all have an effect on each other. They must adapt to work together.
- A budget will take many drafts and lots of compromise.
- Budget for your movie's priorities.
- After making an ideal budget, cut and/or trim every number possible.
- Amend your schedule as necessary to make your budget work.
- Amend your script as necessary to make your budget and schedule work.

Fuck-Up #29

"Post Is Cheap"

Why post far too often gets the short end of the budgeting stick

"Setting a goal is not the main thing. It is deciding how you will go about achieving it and staying with that plan."[7]

—Tom Landry

The Fuck-Up...

A common mistake when budgeting for post-production is that it suffers due to a lack of good planning elsewhere in the budget. Far too often a film goes over budget in pre-production and/or production, so post-production is left to pay the consequences.

How to Do It Right...

The first step to a good post-production budget is having good pre-production and production budgets—and sticking to them. For most movies, production is the stage where you'll burn the most money. But while money is moving quickly, you shouldn't let it all loose on this expensive stage.

You must keep enough saved for post-production, and you must truly appreciate what those costs will entail. Just because money isn't burning as quickly in post as in production does not mean significant expenses aren't in store. How many weeks will you be in the edit? How many people will you be hiring, and what rentals will you be incurring during this time? What are your plans for musical score? Will there be an online edit? Will you be paying a composer? Will you be paying live musicians to record the score? How much money can you set aside for music rights? What can you budget for sound design, ADR, color correction, and special effects? And perhaps the most difficult question of post: What is the final format for your film?

Many new filmmakers mistakenly think of post just as the edit and fail to really consider all the costs actually involved. To begin to appreciate some of the expenses you'll be paying for in post, let's look at some of the costs you may need to pay for during the process (a more complete budget you can use is available at filmmakerfups.com).

See Figure 29.1 and think about this list carefully. If you want to be able to do any or all of these things, they must be budgeted for. Remember that people such as your director and producer continue working through post and are likely to want to get paid for that work (even if they're no longer working on the project exclusively). You may even need your actors for looping or your D.P. for color correction (discussed later in *"Fuck-Up #62: "Cinematography Happens While Shooting"*), so a lot of the rates you established for these individuals in production are likely to still apply.

Post has to be mapped out with a game plan just like production for you to have a realistically functioning budget. And like all well-laid plans, it must have room to adapt to changing

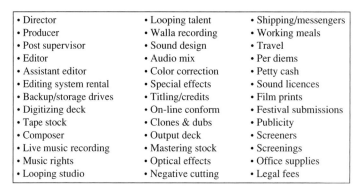

• Director	• Looping talent	• Shipping/messengers
• Producer	• Walla recording	• Working meals
• Post supervisor	• Sound design	• Travel
• Editor	• Audio mix	• Per diems
• Assistant editor	• Color correction	• Petty cash
• Editing system rental	• Special effects	• Sound licences
• Backup/storage drives	• Titling/credits	• Film prints
• Digitizing deck	• On-line conform	• Festival submissions
• Tape stock	• Clones & dubs	• Publicity
• Composer	• Output deck	• Screeners
• Live music recording	• Mastering stock	• Screenings
• Music rights	• Optical effects	• Office supplies
• Looping studio	• Negative cutting	• Legal fees

Figure 29.1 *Overview of Post Costs.*

circumstances. It's not uncommon for new filmmakers to spend much longer than expected to get their movies through all of post-production. Also, a fair amount of technical and other setbacks may occur, so your budget must (as always) allow for a contingency (we'll get into contingencies deeper in the next *Fuck-Up*).

As with all budgeting steps, you have to do your homework to find the best deals on quality labor and services. Comparison shop and see what prices best fit the needs of your film. And remember everything is negotiable.

Quite often, post is simply underbudgeted. This is in part due largely to the digital age of filmmaking. It is possible to do much of post-production inexpensively; however, you're still likely to incur several unavoidable and necessary expensive steps in your post process. Even if you edit and sound design inexpensively in home digital systems, think about color correction, looping, music, visual effects, and final delivery (we'll discuss each of these in more detail in later *Fuck-Ups*). Whenever possible, leave enough breathing room in your post-production budget to make sure your movie can make it through to the end and do so with the quality it deserves. You've worked far too hard to make a good movie to lower the bar for quality late in the game.

Key Points

- The budget left for post often suffers due to poor budgeting or planning during pre-production and production.
- Have a clear plan and budget for post from the beginning of your filmmaking process.
- Reserve a decent portion of your budget for post—enough to accomplish your plan all the way through to the end and cover further unforeseen expenses.
- Think carefully about what costs you'll incur in post. Remember, there's much more than just editing to pay for at this stage.
- Comparison shop to find the best quality deals.
- Doing things digitally and inexpensively works for many steps of the post-production process, but not all of them.

Fuck-Up #30

"I Don't Need a Contingency"

Why you absolutely must budget for a contingency

"The best laid plans of mice and men often go astray."[8]

—Robert Burns

The Fuck-Up...

Contingency is the portion of the budget reserved for unforeseen expenses. Many inexperienced filmmakers are reluctant to put a decent contingency into their budgets. They see keeping this number low as a way to keep down their overall budget. This naïve mistake is incredibly dangerous and can cost you your movie.

> **THE LINGO**
>
> **Contingency:** Money set aside in the budget to cover unforeseen expenses.
>
> Example: Some people say "the contingency is like a life boat." This is a good metaphor, if you think of *every* movie as the Titanic in that you're guaranteed to drown without one.

How to Do It Right...

A generous contingency will save your movie. You may not believe me yet; you may have even already made a budget and cut the contingency. This is a very common rookie mistake and one you will regret deeply. I promise you that if you put in a healthy contingency, when your movie is finished and you look back, you'll think I had the magical power to see the future and predict just how desperately you would need your contingency.

Inexperienced people will frequently pose the question, "Well, what's the contingency for?" To this, a more sane person would respond, "I don't know, and that is exactly what it's for." If this explanation sounds like a contradiction, it is not. In fact, that is the entire point of the contingency. You don't know what you will need that money for, but there are *always* unforeseen expenses and thus you *will* need it.

The standard rule of thumb is that the contingency should be no less than 10 percent of your budget. If you decide to break every other rule outlined in this book, do yourself a favor and make this the one rule you abide by. Make your contingency at least 10 percent of your budget (more if you can). I am more confident that you will need your contingency than I am that the sun will come up tomorrow. Budget for the contingency and you can thank me later.

Those less experienced may budget with items in mind they would like to spend the contingency on, but they are missing the point. If you're thinking "Well, I didn't budget for *X*, so that can come out of the contingency," then you've already fucked up. The contingency is for *unforeseen* expenses. If an expense is foreseen, that means you should budget for it properly.

Key Points

- Contingency is the portion of the budget reserved for unforeseen expenses.
- The contingency is the most important part of your budget and will save your movie.
- The fact that you "can't imagine what you'll need the contingency for" does not change the fact that you absolutely will need it. In fact, its unforeseeable nature is the entire point of the contingency.
- Make your contingency at least 10 percent of your total budget.
- Do not count on paying for foreseeable expenses with the contingency. Reserve it for truly unforeseeable expenses.

Acting

Fuck-Up #31

"Acting Should Always Be Natural"

Why not everything actors do should feel natural

"I love acting. It is so much more real than life."[1]

—Oscar Wilde

The Fuck-Up...

Good acting feels natural. When you watch capable actor perform, it's as if they've become their characters on such a level that the acting ceases to be noticeable and there exists only the characters. However, just because the acting on the screen "feels" natural does not mean the process felt natural while creating it. A common mistake is not appreciating the differences between the process and the performance.

How to Do It Right...

Actors are generally asked to perform with an entire crew watching, under hot lights, and with various on-set dramas unfolding around them. Nevertheless, they must give performances that block all that out and feel natural. The oddity of their surroundings is only part of the less-than-natural factors actors must deal with while performing.

Filmmaking involves a process that is anything but natural to human nature. One example of this that often surprises those new to filmmaking is the sheer amount of repetition required to get a scene filmed. The same scene will likely be performed many times so that it can be shot from different angles, to experiment with slight variations, to give options in the edit, or just for the director's peace of mind. Those new to being on camera are sometimes insulted when asked to do something again and again—not appreciating that this repetition may have nothing to do with the quality of their performance but rather is inherent to the process of filmmaking. Furthermore, it can be difficult for even experienced actors to keep up natural and emotionally committed performances time and again throughout this repetitive process.

If the unusual circumstances and repetition weren't enough, very often scenes will be broken into small pieces, and actors will be asked to redo only part of a scene or even an individual line again and again while maintaining the overall tone of the scene. Scenes have a flow, and it can feel very unnatural to give a line in the middle of a fight, love scene, or joke without what came before it. Nevertheless, this is a common part of an actor's job.

Being able to give natural performances in very unnatural circumstances, again and again, and often broken up into unnaturally small pieces is all part of what makes capable actors so talented. Yet those are not the only "unnatural" skills they must master. Let's discuss a few more....

Camera Awareness

Frequently, new actors will finish a scene and eagerly await feedback only to be told, "I have no idea how your performance was because your back was to the camera most of the time." Experienced actors are always aware of whom they are performing for, whether it is a live audience or, in the case of filmmaking, the camera.

I have seen many passionate young actors so involved in a scene that they completely forget they are obstructing the camera with their backside. In life, there is no camera or audience to consider; thus, it may feel natural for actors to turn their back to the camera if the action calls for it. However, in the world of filmmaking, what is natural is not always what is best.

No matter how magnificent an actor's performance, if the camera can't see it, it's largely lost. Thus, experienced actors maintain a constant sense of camera awareness. This means knowing at all times where the camera is in relation to their performance and adjusting themselves accordingly but never letting that adjustment seem unnatural. Actors with good camera awareness utilize the camera's perspective to showcase their performance in a manner that is appropriate for the scene.

Actors frequently want to "open up" toward the camera; this means that they will angle their actions, movements, and facial expressions to face more toward the camera than they would in "real life" in order to make sure the details are being captured. Opening up to the camera may feel unnatural at times. However, it is up to the director and actors to decide how much they can "cheat the performance to camera" without it appearing unnatural on film. You would be surprised how much opening up you can get away with before it begins to feel unnatural on camera (even if it feels unnatural in life). Watch some sitcom dinner scenes and notice that frequently everyone is sitting on only one side of the table—something that would feel awkward in real life but is rarely questioned when seen on-screen. This is so that at all times the audience can see all the necessary characters. The same technique is used in

Da Vinci's famous mural painting, *The Last Supper*—odd that no one would sit on the other side of the table, isn't it?

Likewise, adjusting one's body to "close off" to camera can also be a valid creative choice. Playing a scene with an actor's back to camera or his facial expression and body language partially obscured can make for a very interesting shot. Many times filmmakers will have more mysterious characters start with their back to the camera, and when we finally see their faces, the shot creates a reveal.

Regardless of whether you are trying to open up to make sure the camera sees every nuance of a performance, or you prefer the mystery of closing off to camera, the lesson remains the same: they both require a constant state of camera awareness.

Clean Shots versus Dirty Shots

In everyday conversation, people often interrupt each other when talking or talk over each other entirely. Although this may feel natural in life, once again we find that what is natural does not always make sense for shooting purposes. Different types of shots require a different approach for the delivery of the actors' dialogue.

Figure 31.1 shows an example of a "clean shot," and Figure 31.2 shows a "dirty shot."

Figure 31.1 *Clean shot. (Original artwork by Manuel Morgado)*

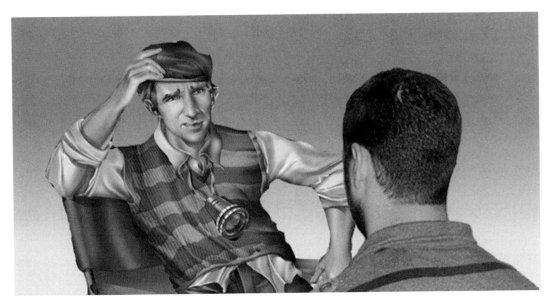

Figure 31.2 *Dirty shot. (Original artwork by Manuel Morgado)*

A "clean shot" means that the only actor in the frame is the one that the shot is designed to feature. In contrast, a "dirty shot" includes at least part of another actor in the scene. Often in a dirty shot, we see the back of the character being spoken to, as is the case in Figure 31.2.

With clean shots, individual shots featuring the different actors will be edited together. So your editor will create any interruptions during a conversation by overlapping the sound from the different shots of each character. However, the editor can create these interruptions only if the dialogue is recorded cleanly, meaning without any real interruptions. Thus, it is preferable that dialogue between actors does not overlap when filming clean shots. This allows the editor to pick which takes she would like to use for each character separately and how much of an interruption to create. Furthermore, even in moments without any interruption, the editor will have the dialogue recorded cleanly if there are no overlaps. This allows the editor to give as much or as little pause as she chooses between lines.

In a dirty shot, in addition to the main actor the shot is featuring, we also see another actor's mannerisms and perhaps even part of his mouth. Thus, it is not necessary for multiple shots to be edited together to get both actors on-screen. Furthermore, it will likely be difficult during overlaps for their performances to be edited apart later. Thus, dialogue and pauses should be delivered naturally as you'd like them to appear in the final edit. A scene involving interruptions should be acted in just that manner—with actors speaking over each other so it all looks natural.

Key Points

- Sometimes actors need to do things that feel unnatural.
- What may feel unnatural while acting a scene can feel fine in the final movie.
- Actors are often asked to perform under odd circumstances and must not let their surroundings hinder their performances.
- Filmmaking involves a lot of repetition.
- Actors will often be asked to break up scenes into very small pieces.
- Actors should always be aware of the camera's location in relation to themselves.
- Actors will often want to "open up" to make sure their performances are done more toward camera.
- In clean shots, actors should not overlap dialogue.
- In dirty shots, dialogue should be natural.

Fuck-Up #32

"Acting Happens When You Have Lines"
Why acting is reacting, even when the camera isn't on

"Acting is paying attention."[2]
—Robert Redford

The Fuck-Up...

Some actors may complain they're not getting enough lines. The misconception here is that talking is when you show you can act.

How to Do It Right...

Amateur actors often make the mistake of waiting for their lines to start acting. More experienced actors, especially those who have spent any time in an editing room, know that acting does not happen only while speaking. In fact, reacting during other actors' lines or action can prove the best way for ambitious actors to get themselves more screen time.

The editor is always looking for effective editing points to help a scene—in other words, something good to cut to. However, if actors are not really acting but just waiting for their turn to speak, they haven't provided any usable reactions to cut to when they are not speaking. But if the actors are constantly reacting, they are giving the editor a lot of usable material. Sometimes in the edit, you might even find that playing the scene on the actor who is reacting is more interesting than playing the scene on the actor who is speaking.

Filmmakers should also be aware that actors are acting regardless of whether or not they're speaking. You must watch your actors at all times, always giving yourself room in the edit to play a scene on a character who's speaking, listening, or doing another action. New filmmakers often obsess over dialogue and neglect that acting is happening constantly. I've seen first-time directors staring intensely at the script during a scene, making sure their actors are getting every word right rather than actually watching the performance. They are neglecting the fact that acting is about a lot more than just getting the lines right.

Furthermore, reacting does not just occur during other people's dialogue. Every moment in a scene is just that, a moment. And a film cannot afford many dull moments. The way characters walk into a room, the way they sip their drink, the way they move to their next mark—none of these are meaningless passing moments (and if they are, they don't belong in the movie to begin with).

THE LINGO

Mark: A marking (tape or otherwise) that shows actors where they are supposed to stand or walk to during a scene.

Example: Peter Falk's iconic staring down while pacing in the TV show *Columbo* was actually Falk trying to find his mark with his one good eye.

Finally, part of good acting is helping other actors improve their own performances. By always acting, performers help other actors have something effective to play off of, better, which, in turn, helps everyone. Actors should never just zone out and wait for their next line. They should always stay in the scene and in character. What may at first seem like "going through the motions" parts almost always provide more opportunities to say something about the character.

Key Points

- Acting does not happen only when speaking.
- The better actors are when they are not speaking, the more they will end up in the final edit.
- Actors, as well as directors, must always pay attention to what all characters are doing in the scene at all times.
- Every moment in a scene is an opportunity to say something about your characters.
- Part of good acting is giving other actors something of quality to work with.

Fuck-Up #33

"Continuity Isn't as Important as Performance"

Why if continuity doesn't match, performance doesn't matter

"Good acting is consistency of performance."[3]

—Jim Dale

The Fuck-Up...

It's your perfect take. The actors are perfect, the light is perfect, the camera work is perfect. Everything is perfect, except in this one take, your star was holding her drink in a different hand than in any of the other shots it will need to cut together with. Guess what? Your perfect take is useless; the continuity error would be too jarring to the audience to use it.

Many people think dealing with continuity is monotonous and thus don't want to bother with it. But without it, your movie will look amateurish or will simply appear to be a "bad movie." Poor continuity is perhaps one of the more famous and more laughable first-timer mistakes.

How to Do It Right...

Continuity refers to making sure everything seen or heard is consistent: a cigarette doesn't suddenly grow or shrink in size between shots; a briefcase doesn't unexpectedly leap from one hand to another; daytime doesn't abruptly become night. The cult movie *The Room* is famous for several bad continuity errors, including at one point having a completely different actor play the same part.

> ### THE LINGO
> **Continuity:** Shot-to-shot consistency.
> Example: Many bad movies are famous for their lack of continuity.

For actors, continuity means consistency in performance. Unfortunately, this is often the most neglected part of most acting classes' curriculums. Many actors would rather focus on performance than consistency, but this reflects a naiveté on how filmmaking works. An actor may have an absolute Oscar-caliber, jaw-dropping, emotionally inspiring take that will forever change your audience's lives. But guess what? If the actor gives that performance standing in a different spot than in the rest of the coverage, that amazing take simply will not cut together with the other footage and thus is useless because of a simple continuity error. Great performance or not, kiss that Oscar goodbye.

Continuity does not refer only to which hand an actor holds a prop in or where he stands. It also has a lot to do with timing, such as crossing the room on the same line take after take or folding his legs on the same beat. I've had to let go of great takes because the time at which one character put a comforting hand on another character's shoulder was inconsistent, and you can't cut between shots where hands are magically jumping around.

Some continuity errors may go largely unnoticed by the audience. However, many will kick an audience out of the movie completely, making their suspension of disbelief difficult. There is, of course, a significant difference between an actor suddenly holding a prop in a different hand versus inexplicably changing wardrobe in the middle of a scene. Nevertheless, any inconsistency runs the risk of limiting what can be used in the final edit. Thus, it is in your best interest to maintain as much continuity as possible.

THE LINGO

Suspension of disbelief: The audience's ability to ignore practical logic in order to enjoy a work of fiction.

Example: Most action movies require a significant suspension of disbelief.

For very experienced actors, continuity is so routine that most don't even need to think about it to remain consistent. In addition, keeping track of continuity is primarily the responsibility of the script supervisor. And, although it should not be his primary concern, the director should also have a general awareness of continuity.

It is also the director's responsibility to decide when to ignore continuity. As with any good rule, the need for consistency should be selectively ignored. Experimenting with variations can be one of the most phenomenal parts of the filmmaking process. Just be aware: it may limit what you're able to use in the edit. But like Fellini said, "Spontaneity is the secret of life."[4]

Key Points

- Continuity means ensuring consistency between shots and scenes.
- Continuity errors can make footage unusable.
- Continuity is primarily the responsibility of the script supervisor.
- Ignoring continuity for the sake of variation and experimentation can have wonderful benefits.

Crew

Fuck-Up #34

"Hire a D.P. Based on Who Owns a Camera"

What you really should look for in a D.P.

"You are always a student, never a master.
You have to keep moving forward."[1]
—Conrad Hall, legendary D.P.

The Fuck-Up...

There are countless aspiring directors of photography out there. To beat out the competition and get work, many will offer the use of their equipment for little or no cost. As you can imagine, this is a tempting offer for an indie film on a tight budget. However, hiring a director of photography *solely* based on who will give the best deal on equipment is a classic rookie mistake—one that shows an underappreciation of a D.P.'s job and can cost the look your film dearly.

How to Do It Right...

The director of photography, or D.P. (this job used to be called the "cinematographer," but everyone likes having "director" in his or her title), is the primary person, in conjunction with the director, responsible for achieving the visual look of the film. The D.P. oversees the lighting and camerawork on set. As with many set jobs, it is a simple job to define and a vastly technical and artistic job to accomplish. Think of the director as the artist who decides how she wants the painting to look, but is not the actual painter. The director may say she wants the lighting to look "gritty, high contrast, and stark," but how that is accomplished is up to the D.P. and his crew.

The D.P. should be one of the director's closest allies. And if a director is new to feature-filmmaking, the D.P. should be both an ally and perhaps even a crutch to lean on. Get an experienced, artistic D.P. whom you truly trust and are very comfortable with. The D.P.'s control of the visual look of the film can be the difference between your movie looking like a professional film, or an amateur home movie.

Appropriately enough, different directors will work differently with their D.P.s. Often when a director is referred to as an "actor's director," there is an implication that she is so performance focused that she is leaving most of the visual responsibilities to the D.P. This may or may not be true for any given director, but there is no doubt that some directors choose to be much more visually controlling, and some directors defer more of this responsibility to their D.P. Any relationship is fine as long as it works for you and your movie. The key is figuring out how you want to work and finding that appropriate relationship.

When you are choosing D.P.s, there are many factors to consider carefully. Watch their reels to see if their past work shows the talent and competence to accomplish the right look for your film. Discuss style and approach to see if their sensibilities align with that of your movie. Find out if they're comfortable working on films of the same budget size and limitations as yours. Check references to feel out whether they will able to work at whatever pace is necessary for your film. And make sure the D.P. you choose is someone your director is very comfortable having as one of her closest collaborators.

> **THE LINGO**
>
> **Reel:** A video compilation of someone's past work.
>
> Example: Directors, D.P.s, producers, costume designers, production designers, and many other people in the industry will often be asked to show a reel of their past work when being considered for a job.

Competent D.P.s need to be both good employees and good bosses. To accomplish his visual goals, the D.P. oversees three departments that will pick up the metaphorical paint and brushes: the Grip, Electric, and Camera departments.

D.P.s, like directors, are what are sardonically referred to as "white glove" jobs, implying they do not touch the gear. Although this term is sometimes used in jest, having a hands-off director and D.P. is actually a good thing. The director and D.P. have a lot of creative responsibilities, and chances are, if they are off setting a light, they are ignoring something else that needs their attention. I can imagine little on set that would be more frustrating than actors looking for their director, only to find she is out running cable. Likewise, D.P.s rely on the Grip and Electric departments to carry out their goals.

Fuck-Up #35

"Grip? Electric? What's the difference?"

Understanding what grips and electrics do

> "Q: How many grips does it take to change a light bulb?
> A: None. That's an electric's job."
> —author unknown

The Fuck-Up...

Grips and electrics (short for electricians) are commonly thought of collectively as the "G&E department." Although they do work in conjunction with each other, it is a mistake to think of them as the same job. There are important differences in their responsibilities, so to avoid confusing their functions, let's examine what these people do.

How to Do It Right...

Some grips and/or electrics who read this book may be infuriated that they've been lumped into one section together. They are separate jobs and prefer to be thought of as such. However, we can avoid further offending them by understanding their differences.

Electrics, as the name implies, work with things that involve electricity. Their foremost responsibility is powering and lighting the set. They also regulate all other electrical use on set. It is a good rule of thumb that when plugging in anything at all on set, you first check with the Electric department. Do not embarrass yourself by bringing the shoot to a screeching halt because you plugged your hair dryer where you shouldn't and have now caused all the lights to go out.

By contrast, grips work primarily with what does not require electricity. This includes, but is not limited to, stands, dollies, flags, jibs, cranes, and other rigging. The grips work hand in hand with the electrics. If a light needs to be placed on a rig, the grips build the rig, and the electrics place and power the light. If a light's intensity needs to be reduced, the grips would place the flag or diffusion that does so. Another way to think of this is: electrics add light, grips take light away.

The "key grip" heads the Grip department, and the "gaffer" (sometimes called "the chief lighting technician") heads the Electric department. The key grip and gaffer will meet with the D.P. to discuss the D.P.'s plan. The D.P. may give very specific instructions on how to light a scene, right down to what type of light to put where, or instead more general direction as to the overall look and then allow the gaffer and key grip to work out the details.

The gaffer and key grip have their own crew to help execute the plan. Working below them will be their departments' second in command, called "best boys." The gaffer's second is called "best boy electric," and the key grip's second is "best boy grip." After the "bests," numbers are generally attached to denote where they stand in their hierarchy: third grip, fourth electric, and so on. There is also sometimes what is called a "swing," and this is someone who may help fill in either on the grip or electric side as needed.

An important side note about key grips is that, in conjunction with the 1st A.D. (who is in charge of overseeing all on-set happenings), they are responsible for on-set safety. For example, if a rig seems unsafe for an actor to stand on, it is the key grip's responsibility to voice concern and not allow any unsafe practices to occur.

Key Points

- Grips and electrics work together but have different responsibilities.
- Electrics are responsible for all lighting and powering requirements on set.
- Grips are in charge of all rigging, including camera and dolly rigs, flags, apple boxes, stands, jibs, and cranes.
- The key grip heads the Grip department.
- The gaffer heads the Electric department.
- The key grip's and gaffer's second in command are called their "best boys."
- The key grip, along with the 1st A.D., is responsible for safety on set.

Fuck-Up #36

"The Assistant Director Is the Director's Assistant"

What this crucial job really does and why you need a great one

"The first assistant director is just so important that the choice of that person is critical to the movie."[2]

—John Frankenheimer

The Fuck-Up...

Allow me to eliminate a popular misconception: the assistant director is absolutely not the director's assistant. It is a misleading title that in no way, shape, or form involves fetching the director's coffee, answering the phone, picking up dry cleaning, or doing anything else commonly thought of as "assistant" work. Nevertheless, the assistant director is absolutely of indispensable assistance to the director.

It is a tremendous mistake for new filmmakers to underappreciate the assistant director's role. It can prevent them from utilizing the A.D. in a manner that will ensure the set runs efficiently. Furthermore, by understanding what an A.D. does, a good director or producer can help support the A.D. in a manner that will help him do his job better, which in turn will benefit the entire shoot immeasurably.

How to Do It Right...

In short, the 1st assistant director (1st A.D.) is in charge of running the set. The 1st A.D. creates the schedule, manages the set, makes sure work is performed in a timely and efficient manner, and ensures that everyone is informed as to what's happening—with the big goal of getting all the day's scheduled work accomplished.

Having all this responsibility also means should anything happen to cause the shoot to go off schedule, the 1st A.D. is likely to get blamed. As the old joke goes, "If it rains, that's the A.D.'s fault."

To scratch the surface of what the job entails, here are some of the 1st A.D.'s responsibilities:

- Set schedules.
- Make sure filming stays on schedule as much as possible.

- Set cast and crew call times.
- Disseminate necessary information to keep cast and crew informed.
- Decide when the crew will break for meals.
- Control walkie-talkie communication.
- Call the roll (this means calling "roll sound," "roll camera," "action," and so on, to inform everyone of the shooting protocol).
- Limit and enforce the amount of time allotted for every setup and shot.
- Manage the director's time and who has access to her (everyone thinks that they need to talk to the director; most are mistaken).
- Manage the personalities of the cast and crew to help avoid or handle any potential conflicts.
- And, work on the front line of the never-ending battle to get the director what she wants.

Many people view 1st A.D.s as the set dictators. Sometimes they're even referred to as the "set drill sergeants" and are forced to take on a more villainous persona to get things done. Different 1st A.D.s have different styles, which may or may not require a "villain" role on the set. Any A.D. will tell you it is not an easy job and often requires extreme approaches. A set can move or not move based on the 1st A.D.'s ability to give it momentum. Following the director (and on some sets, the stars), the 1st A.D. is the person who is most likely to set the tone.

Another far-too-common and always deeply regrettable mistake new filmmakers make is thinking they don't need an A.D. at all. However, anyone with any real filmmaking experience knows that a good A.D. department saves a production far more money than it costs. The quality of your A.D. department is one of the key factors that will decide how successful your shoot goes, what the tone on the set will be, and how much work gets successfully accomplished every day. Without a good 1st A.D., most sets quickly fall into something resembling complete chaos. It is crucial that you hire a 1st A.D. who is capable at creating and effectively managing the schedule and running your set in the manner you want and need it run.

The 1st A.D. is the head of the A.D. department, which may also include a 2nd A.D., 2nd 2nd A.D., and 3rd A.D.s. These people support the 1st A.D. both on and off the set by making sure everything is happening to schedule, information is being dispersed, call sheets are being made and distributed, company moves happen efficiently, talent is well managed, and much more. The 1st A.D. is also in charge of all on-set P.A.s, who do a ton of work (which we'll discuss in more detail in *Fuck-Up #37: "Anyone Can Be a P.A."*)

> **THE LINGO**
>
> **Company move:** A change in location that requires all the cast, crew, vehicles, and equipment to be moved.
>
> Example: The company move took three hours: one hour to pack up, one hour to drive to the new location, and one hour to unload and set up again.

> ## Key Points
> - An assistant director is in no way a director's assistant.
> - The 1st assistant director runs the set.
> - The 1st A.D. is responsible for making and keeping the schedule.
> - The A.D. department keeps the cast and crew informed as to the schedule and its changes.
> - The 1st A.D. will likely get blamed if anything at all causes filming to go off schedule.
> - Many people view A.D.s as the on-set villains (and in some cases they're right).
> - A set without a good 1st A.D. is likely to fall into chaos.
> - The 1st A.D. is in charge of the rest of the A.D.s as well as set P.A.s.

Fuck-Up #37

"Anyone Can Be a P.A."

What it really takes to pull off this difficult job effectively

"Executive ability is deciding quickly and getting somebody else
to do the work."[3]
—John G. Pollard

The Fuck-Up...

When someone is just starting out working on film sets, there is an excellent chance his first job will be as a "production assistant" (better known as a "P.A."). Since this job is at the bottom of the crew hierarchy, it's often mistakenly thought of as an "anyone can do it" kind of job. Assuming that a P.A. doesn't require intelligence, ability, and training is a serious misstep that can leave your set with a complete lack of functioning support.

How to Do It Right...

"Hey, my son/daughter/friend/friend's kid wants to work in movies; maybe you could make him a P.A. or something?" is a request many filmmakers are likely to hear.

It is common for someone loosely involved in a production to mention a friend or relative who is interested in film and ask if that person can "be a P.A." For this reason, do not be surprised if you find yourself hiring some P.A.s as political hires. Although this is not always a bad thing, it represents a basic misunderstanding of what it takes to be a good P.A.

> **THE LINGO**
> **Political hire:** Someone hired for reasons other than his abilities.

Production assistants can exist in all departments (Grip P.A.s, Art P.A.s, Office P.A.s, etc.). The term "P.A." has simply come to imply the lowest paid position in each department's hierarchy ("interns" are lower in the hierarchy but generally unpaid). The most common kind of P.A., those simply called "P.A." or "set P.A.," works under the A.D. department's supervision on set, and that is the kind we'll be discussing here.

P.A.s are responsible for many crucial tasks. Common duties include but are certainly not limited to:

- "Locking up" locations. They protect the set so that random passersby do not disrupt work.
- "Echoing the 1st A.D." They inform everyone when the 1st A.D. has called out things such as "quiet," "rolling," "cutting," "going again," and "moving on." This helps inform the cast and crew what is going on at all times.

> **THE LINGO**
> **Lock-ups:** P.A.s are placed strategically throughout a location to control the space and any passersby.
> Example: Lock-ups in New York City are a surefire way to anger the locals.

- Literally RUNNING to get whatever item the set may be waiting on.
- Helping set up and break down meals, production offices, and other equipment.
- Doing anything else at all that may be required. Stuff always rolls downhill, so be assured it will stop at a P.A. If something needs to be swept, cleaned, picked up, dropped off, driven, moved, remembered, forgotten, or taken care of, "get a P.A."

Very often, new P.A.s will not appreciate the amount of work (or type of work) they are signing up for. When making "political hires," decide whether you can give real P.A. work to these people, or perhaps you need to find some less intensive job to give them and leave the more difficult work to P.A.s with experience. If you are forced to hire P.A.s based on politics and not ability, make sure you have at least a few strong and experienced P.A.s on board to help pick up the slack. It's fine to be training a few new P.A.s on a shoot, but if they all lack experience, it can be difficult and time consuming to train everyone.

On medium to large sized sets, all P.A. duties are given to the head P.A., called the "key P.A.," to delegate. The key P.A. must keep track of which P.A.s are doing what tasks and then assign new tasks to an available P.A. of her choosing.

In addition to their assigned duties, good P.A.s will constantly be looking for ways to be of service and help the set run better. It's a difficult and demanding job that takes tremendous hunger, dedication, and intelligence to do well, and thus not just anyone who's available can do it. P.A.s are most likely to be the first to arrive on set and the last to leave every day.

Like most on-set jobs, being a P.A. likely involves large chunks of downtime, but when a P.A. is needed, his ability to handle a task quickly and effectively makes the difference between a well-run set and an out-of-control nightmare.

Key Points

- P.A. (production assistant) is the most common entry-level position on set.
- P.A. jobs should not simply be given out to any newcomer in film.
- All departments can have P.A.s.
- Set P.A.s perform a long list of crucial tasks.
- Work that rolls downhill likely stops at a P.A.
- The key P.A. is in charge of all the set P.A.s.
- Being a good P.A. takes a lot of hard work, intelligence, and dedication.
- Good P.A.s are the backbone of a well-run set.

Fuck-Up #38

"We Don't Need an Art Department"
What these people really do and why you really need them

"Any time you talk about the look of the film, it's not just the director and the director of photography. You have to include the costume designer and the production designer."[4]

—Spike Lee

The Fuck-Up...

Some new filmmakers view their art department needs as relatively minimal and thus attempt to go at it without an official art department. However, they quickly discover this job is a lot more work than they fully appreciated and are left scrambling to pick up the slack left by not having the right people on board to focus on their art department needs. Worse yet, their movie is now suffering from this mistake both behind the camera and in front of it.

How to Do It Right...

The art department is responsible for finding or building all sets, set dressing, props, and scenery you see in a movie. This can mean anything from creating an entire other world from scratch to utilizing found items in a pre-existing location.

The art department is as important to the look of your movie as any other element involved. Having a good art department devoted to this important job will help raise the quality of your film to a higher level.

To better understand the art department, let's look at the people who run it.

Production Designer

The production designer is responsible for designing the look of all the sets. First, he or she works closely with the director to conceive how every set should look and feel. Then the production designer leads the art department in designing and achieving that vision. This includes constructing and decorating sets, acquiring props and furniture, and so on.

A production designer often works well ahead of the shooting crew, prepping the next day's, week's, or even the next month's sets depending on the scope of the project. Because the production designer is constantly trying to stay ahead of the shooting crew, he often cannot be on set for what is being filmed. Thus, the production designer has a team of on-set people to rely upon to help see out his and the director's collective vision.

Art Director

Because the production designer spends much of his time preparing for the future, the art director is left to deal more directly with the present. The art director is the foremost person responsible for aiding the production designer and making sure the plan is adhered to in the designer's absence.

The art director helps determine the dressing, scenery, and props to best compliment the set. The art director also leads the rest of the on-set art department, including all set dressers as well as the props department.

Set Dressers versus Prop Masters

While set dressers and prop masters both work in the art department and help decorate the set, there is a very specific delineation as to where their responsibilities fall. The easy way to tell the difference is if an actor moves it, it is a "prop." And if an actor doesn't move it, it's "set dressing." So let's say there's a lamp in a scene. If the lamp sits there untouched during the scene, it is "set dressing," and a set dresser is in charge of it. However, if an actor picks up the lamp, it becomes a "prop" and a prop master is now in charge of it. Whoever's in charge will pick out the item; that person will either design or build it and will be in charge of it while on set.

Set dressers are responsible for all the furniture, drapes, wallpaper, and the countless other "dressings" that a scene may involve. And "props" (short for prop masters) are similarly in charge of the umbrellas, handguns, telephones, and any other props a given scene requires. This means they are also in charge of "resetting" after each take, meaning whatever moved during the shot gets put back to where it was, so it can be ready for another take. If, during a shot, a prop gets moved, a glass gets filled, or the set gets covered in snow, it will need to be reset by the art department in order to get ready for another take. The art department's ability to reset quickly can be one of the key factors in how efficiently the clock is managed.

Key Points

- The art department is very important, and its responsibilities should not be underestimated.
- The art department, along with the director and D.P., is largely responsible for creating the "look" of a movie.
- The production designer is the head of the art department and the one responsible for designing the on-screen look of all locations, sets, set dressing, and props.
- The art director is responsible for making sure the production designer's vision is executed on set.
- Set dressers and property masters both work in the art department but have different responsibilities.
- The art department must efficiently reset the set dressing and props as necessary after every take.

Fuck-Up #39

"I Don't Need a Script Supervisor"

Why not having a script supervisor is dangerous

"Beware of the person who can't be bothered by details."[5]

—William Feather

The Fuck-Up...

Remember which hand your actor used to reach for his glass in the master shot from yesterday? How about the shirt he was wearing in the scene you shot five weeks ago? Or what the scar looked like on his cheek in your favorite take? Guess what? With a good script supervisor, you don't have to remember any of that. Small details such as these are tremendously important, and a script supervisor lives in detail.

New filmmakers sometimes fail to appreciate the importance of a script supervisor—that is, until they get to the editing room and realize the countless mistakes a good script supervisor would have helped them avoid.

How to Do It Right...

The job of script supervisor has evolved to include so many tasks that a job description could easily be its own book. However, for our simpler goal of convincing you why you desperately need a professional script supervisor, let's look at just an overview of the script supervisor's duties.

Notes

The script supervisor takes detailed notes on every take. This is the written record your post-production crew utilizes to know what occurred on set: which takes the director liked, what setup they were on, who flubbed a line, where the camera ran out of film, what lens was used, and anything else that went either right or wrong.

These notes will be turned into the "Daily Editor's Log" and "Daily Production Report." Figure 39.1 shows a part of a Daily Editor's Log from my film *Made for Each Other*, created by the wonderful script supervisor Jodi Domanic-Riccio. The circles mark the takes the director likes as a signal to the editor that those should be looked at closely. (You can find samples of Daily Editor's Logs and Daily Production Reports you can use for your own film at filmmakerfups.com.)

117

DAILY EDITOR'S LOG
Made For Each Other

Day: 1

Date: 08/05/2007

State	Take #	Description	CR	SR	Time	Lens	Comments	SU
41	1	H/H, med ots of DAN on ASSISTANT	A1	1	1:13	16	Good until mack walk away	1
41	2	H/H, med ots of DAN on ASSISTANT	A1	1	1:15	16	Good had hug for walk away. Didn't want hug at very end though. Sound issue.	1
41	3	H/H, med ots of DAN on ASSISTANT	A1	1	1:16	16	Good. No hug this time	1
41	4 PU	H/H, med ots of DAN on ASSISTANT	A1	1	0:35	16	Went to lighter 2 shot for DAN end of scene. From mack's entrance to end. Great, especially Dan very end.	1
41A	1	H/H, med leads DAN into ots on DAN. At end MACK walks away go to ots of dan on MACK	A1	1	1:28	16	Pretty good but 1week bkgd	2

Figure 39.1 *Portion of a Daily Editor's Log. (Created by script supervisor Jodi Domanic-Riccio)*

Continuity

The script supervisor must maintain a retentive eye for continuity from shot to shot, day to day, week to week, and month to month. If an actor needs to recall which way her legs were folded on the previous take or even the previous scene shot three months ago, it will be the script supervisor's job to remind the actor. All continuity from what time wall clocks should read to an actor's movements must be carefully tracked and noted by the script supervisor. Thus, every good script supervisor should be armed with meticulous notes, a good memory, and a digital camera.

Lining Scripts

The system by which the script supervisor annotates what portions of the script have been filmed by what shots is called "lining scripts." A lined script has a shot number with a line below it covering the portion of the script that shot covered.

Figure 39.2 shows an excerpt from a sample lined script. A straight line is for dialogue and action covered facing camera, and a zigzag line denotes what's been covered either off-camera or not featuring that character. These lined scripts serve as a great tool for both the director and editor to know what shots have covered what portions of a scene. An editor will use this tool if she needs to know if a moment is covered in any other shots. And for a director, it is a great reference tool as to what has been accomplished, what sort of coverage already exists, and what should be accomplished next.

Dialogue Changes

The script supervisor keeps records of all dialogue changes and can help inform the actors of any changes to the script or misspoken dialogue. These changes will also be noted in the script supervisor's lined version of the script.

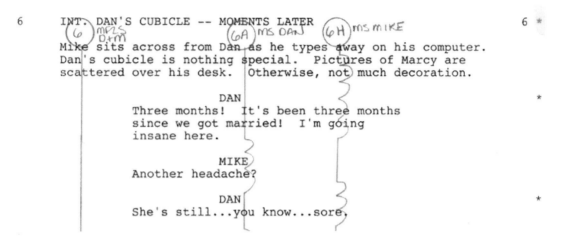

Figure 39.2 *Sample lined script. (Script written by screenwriter Eric Lord and lined by script supervisor Jodi Domanic-Riccio)*

Shot Numbering

The script supervisor is in charge of numbering every shot and individual take. He must make sure the 2nd A.C. (assistant camera) and sound mixer are aware of what shot number they are filming at all times so that the slate and their reports can match appropriately. If these elements do not match, it can cause tremendous confusion in post-production organization.

THE LINGO

Slate: The thing that gets clapped right after the camera starts rolling and before the director calls "action." It has information written on it regarding what is being shot (the scene, shot, take, director, D.P., etc.) to inform the editor what she is looking at. The clapping action helps in the synchronization of the picture and sound later in post-production.

Line Feeding

Some actors want to be prompted if they are struggling to remember a line. It is the responsibility of the script supervisor to provide these "line feedings."

Line Readings

If an actor is performing his side of a conversation without a fellow actor present to provide the other side, the script supervisor will deliver the missing actor's lines. A common example is when filming one side of a phone call, the script supervisor will read the lines of the character who is supposed to be on the other end.

Running Time

The script supervisor keeps notes on the running time of each shot. This helps estimate the total running times of scenes and project the running time of the movie. This information is especially crucial if a scene or piece of dialogue needs to fit into a specific duration.

Coverage

The script supervisor may suggest coverage if he feels that a line or action has not been filmed and thus will be lacking in the final edit.

Eyelines

The script supervisor keeps track of which way characters are looking when they address each other. This way, when there is a cut between actors, all the actors appear to be looking at who (or what) they're supposed to be.

Daily Logs

The script supervisor produces daily logs that summarize what portions of the movie were successfully filmed on each day and what scheduled portions were not accomplished and are thus "owed" (meaning they will need to be rescheduled).

It's easy to see the many ways a script supervisor is indispensable. A good script supervisor will save you time, money, and aggravation. So it is worth investing in someone capable and experienced. Whether you are shooting a 30-second commercial with no dialogue or a feature-film with lots of dialogue, a good script supervisor is an asset to any production.

Key Points

- Script supervisors perform a long list of crucial functions.
- Script supervisors keep diligent notes, keep track of continuity and shot numbering, know all dialogue changes, perform line feedings and readings, measure running times, line the script, make sure all your action is properly covered, keep track of actors' eyelines, and keep daily logs.
- The job of script supervisor should not be given to someone inexperienced.
- If you're not sure whether you need a script supervisor, you need a script supervisor.

Fuck-Up #40

"Set Photographers Don't Help the Movie"

Why preparing promotional material is as important as the movie itself

"Advertising is totally unnecessary. Unless you hope to make money."[6]
—Jef I. Richards

The Fuck-Up...

Set photographers are hired to take photographs that will be used to help promote the film to distributors and audiences. Some new filmmakers are quick to cut them from the budget because they view the movie as the highest priority and set photographers are not involved in the actual making of the movie itself. However, anyone who has been through the process of delivering a film to distributors will tell you this is a big mistake—one that may prevent your film from getting distributed.

How to Do It Right...

If you're making an independent film, there is a good chance you will not have distribution in place prior to commencing shooting. When it comes time to sell and promote your movie, you will quickly realize how tremendously important promotional materials are—and the necessity for set photos to help create them.

To raise distributors' interest in your film, you often have to do a good amount of their job for them and that means proving that the film is actually marketable. If you can make impressive posters, a website, and/or an electronic press kit (EPK), you are much more likely to sell your movie. In fact, many movies sell based on their posters and trailers, even before the movie itself gets seen.

In the age of online promotion, you will also need a lot of content for online campaigns, whether it be on Facebook, fan sites, or elsewhere. That means photos, behind-the-scenes videos, cast and crew interviews, and whatever else you can come up with to help build audience interest and awareness. All that content must be produced, and that means having on-set photographers and videographers whose purpose is not to help make the movie, but to help promote it.

Even after you sell your movie, you will have a long list of "deliverables" the distributor will require to help further market the film. If you don't fulfill your deliverables, the distributor can reject the film and choose not to release it at all. A multitude of high-quality set photos featuring the cast (drunken pictures of the crew don't interest them) is a standard required deliverable for any distributor.

Some filmmakers who made their movies without set photographers are left scrambling to fulfill this delivery requirement, attempting to take these photos well after filming is over. However, they often find that getting their cast, sets, wardrobe, and so on back together after filming is finished to be virtually impossible. So why risk it? Aim to acquire your set photos and behind-the-scenes materials all while making the film itself.

To keep down costs, set photographers and behind-the-scenes videographers do not need to be on set everyday. Plan strategically to have them around during the shooting that is most likely to give you the best marketing materials. Think about what the marketing of your movie might be like and make sure you have a photographer around on the necessary days to capture it. It may be the days you have most of your actors or your most famous actors on set. It may be the days with your biggest set pieces, action sequences, or climaxes. And as always, leave yourself options. Although it's certainly not necessary to have the photographer around every day, you're better off having her there too much than not enough. Often you don't know when that magical moment that will make your film's marketing campaign will unfold, so help fate's odds by giving it more opportunities to strike.

Key Points

- Getting publicity materials such as photos and behind-the-scenes material is very important to the sale, distribution, and marketing of a film.
- Publicity materials can be as crucial to a film's success as the movie itself (if not more so).
- You have to show distributors that your film is marketable by having already created effective marketing materials for it.
- You will need a lot of promotional materials for your film's online marketing campaign.
- You will be contractually required to provide your distributor with set photos.
- It can be difficult to re-create scenes from your film later, so get your promotional materials during shooting.
- A set photographer and behind-the-scenes videographer do not need to be present during every day of shooting. Pick which days will provide the best material for marketing purposes.

Fuck-Up #41

"Sound Is Not Important"

Why this is the dumbest thing you may ever hear on set

"A beautiful thing never gives so much pain as does failing to hear and see it."[7]
—Michelangelo

The Fuck-Up...

Have you ever been watching a movie and then got up and walked into another room so you could only hear the TV but not see it? Chances are, by merely hearing the movie, you could still follow much of what was going on. Now try watching the same movie on mute and see how much you can follow.

The truth is that the lion's share of your story is more than likely to be told via sound. The dialogue, the music, and the mood are all built largely in the audience's ears. And yet those naïve to filmmaking still think of it as primarily a "visual medium." This mentality means they are prone to vastly underappreciate sound's importance. If your sound is bad, no matter how great the writing, directing, acting, or visuals, the audience will simply be incapable of enjoying your film.

How to Do It Right...

"Let's go see a movie" may be the figure of speech, but have no doubt what the audience really wants is an experience for both their eyes and ears to enjoy. Furthermore, an audience is far more willing to tolerate poor picture quality than even mediocre sound quality. Many terribly shot movies went on to achieve success, but the soundtrack was still clear (Kevin Smith's *Clerks* and Paul Provenza's *The Aristocrats* are both examples of this phenomenon of poorly shot movies with good sound that achieved success). I challenge you to find any example in which the opposite is true: a movie that was beautifully shot but the sound was terrible and yet it still went on to achieve success. Even filmmakers of ultra low-budget successes like Robert Rodriguez's *El Mariachi* may have spent only eight thousand dollars shooting the film, but the distributor spent hundreds of thousands fixing the soundtrack to get it to a releasable quality that audiences would tolerate.

Time and again, it's been proven that what is most important to an audience, whether they realize it or not, is having good sound quality. To avoid annoying your audience and making it impossible for them to enjoy your movie, you must prioritize your film's sound quality.

Although the "sound department" may be one of the smaller departments in terms of staffing, it is of the utmost importance on set. With that point in mind, let's examine the role of the technicians who will determine the quality of sound recorded on set.

Sound Mixer

The sound mixer has the critical duty of being ultimately responsible for all sound recorded on set. The term "mixer" is a bit misleading, because actually mixing the levels of the multiple microphones being used is only one important part of this person's responsibilities. The sound mixer must also decide what microphone placement will provide the optimal sound recording for every scene and its unique challenges. Just as there are infinite places to put the camera to shoot any given scene, there are infinite ways to mic a scene. A good sound mixer will examine the set, the actors' movements and wardrobe, and the scene as a whole to figure out where to place microphones to provide the best sound quality possible.

When you are hiring a sound mixer, it is absolutely vital not to simply hire the person who offers the best rate or equipment. Choosing a poor sound mixer can cost you far more money and frustration in post-production, where you'll be left with poor quality or unusable sound and have to struggle to fix the problem. Poorly recorded sound may even make your movie unreleasable.

Boom Operator

The boom operator works under the sound mixer's guidance to operate the boom microphone.

Boom operator is one of those jobs that everyone seems to think he can do, until he actually has to do it and discover it

THE LINGO

Boom: The roving microphone on top of a long pole that the operator can move along with the actors.

is vastly more difficult than it looks. A good boom operator not only needs the physical agility to operate a boom over his head for a long period of time, but also the mental capacity to anticipate every line of dialogue that is going to be spoken. Good boom operators study the scene closely and know when every character will speak so they can be ready with the microphone accordingly. I've been on sets where if actors blank on a line, the boom operator is the person they turn to because he knows the dialogue better than anyone. Furthermore, the boom operator must perform this function with a ninja (yes "ninja") like precision to avoid causing any sound interference with his hands, which the boom mic will pick up. If a boom operator cannot maintain a majestically gentle touch for extended periods of time, the sound he picks up will suffer greatly.

Key Points

- Most of your story will likely be told via the sound, not the picture.
- Audiences are vastly more likely to tolerate poor picture quality than even mediocre sound quality.
- Movies are *not* primarily a visual medium.
- Having poor sound recorded on set will cost you immensely more money in post-production to fix.
- Sound mixers are in charge of designing the microphone placement for a scene.
- Boom operator is one of those jobs that everyone seems to think he can do until he actually has to do it.
- Sound is of equal importance to picture, if not more so.

Life on Set

Fuck-Up #42

"The Director Should Worry about Everything"
Why the director should be kept in the dark about most problems

"Hire people who are better than you are; then leave them to get on with it."[1]
—David Ogilvy

The Fuck-Up...

First-time directors often think they need to worry about EVERYTHING: where's lunch, is the wardrobe going to be ready on time, is the truck fixed yet, is my crew happy, am I going over budget, did the dailies make it to the lab, and so on. They see the entire movie as their baby and that they (like many first-time parents) must control everything that influences their child. However, even new parents eventually learn that while it might be their baby, it is going to take a village to raise it.

Thousands of problems will arise while making a movie, but 99 percent of them should not be the director's worry. In fact, the director should not even be aware of most of the problems that other people deal with to keep the movie going day-to-day. The director must be able to focus almost entirely on the demanding and important task of directing. Any attempts to divide his or her attention, necessary or not, will likely come at a cost to the film.

How to Do It Right...

THE DIRECTOR NEEDS TO CONCENTRATE ON DIRECTING.

The saying goes "A success is everyone's accomplishment. A failure is the director's fault." Directing a film is indeed a difficult job with a lot of pressure. Directors must always be imagining their film—they must simultaneously focus on the small pieces within the film, as well as envision how those pieces will make-up the overall film as a whole. In addition to imagining the film, the director must be able to effectively communicate that vision to the cast and crew helping to execute it. However, outside distractions that do not strictly relate to the directing of the movie are likely to spread the director's attention thin, and that means the director isn't focusing enough on an already-demanding and high-pressure job.

You hire a crew for a reason. Directors should hire good people, trust them to be on top of the many issues they need to be on top of, and train themselves to let go. A director can and should check in often but should not feel obligated to micromanage. A big part of the crew's job is to handle things in a manner that leaves the director free as much as possible. On a professional set, every effort is made to keep the director in the dark regarding any problems he or she does not absolutely need to know about. If a problem can be handled without bringing it to the director's attention, it should be. Furthermore, most professional directors appreciate their forced state of naiveté to most of the set's problems as it leaves them free to focus on their real job—envisioning the movie and communicating that vision to the cast and crew that will help bring it to life.

There are, of course, countless questions that must be brought to the director's attention, and a director will spend a very large portion of every day answering such questions: How should a piece of wardrobe look? What color should the walls be painted? How will a scene be filmed? What is the character thinking in this scene? And so on and so on and so on. But to give the director enough time to field the questions he or she should be answering (those that pertain to the vision of the movie and how to execute it), the crew must spare the director the questions that do not demand such attention.

Key Points

- The director should not attempt to worry about everything.
- Most problems do not need the director's attention.
- The director's real job is to (1) envision the movie and (2) communicate that vision to the people who will help bring it to life.
- The director must trust her crew to handle problems.
- The director should be kept in the dark about every problem that does not absolutely demand her attention.
- The more the director can focus solely on directing issues, the more the movie will benefit.

Fuck-Up #43

"It's Quick On-Screen; It Shouldn't Take Long to Shoot"

Why screen time has little correlation to shooting time

"Make the hard ones look easy and the easy ones look hard."[2]

—Walter Hagen

The Fuck-Up...

Those new to film sets often show up expecting a great deal of glamour and excitement, and after a while of not much happening, they often leave bored. Although movies are designed to make what appears on the screen interesting, exciting, dramatic, romantic, and so on, that does not mean any of these feelings are reflective of what occurred off-screen while making the film.

Likewise, although a movie may be made to feel well paced on-screen, shooting it rarely ever is. Where many new filmmakers go wrong is in believing that screen time is an accurate indication of shooting time.

How to Do It Right...

On the "The Ultimate Edition DVD" for *Terminator 2: Judgment Day* (which is apparently not the most ultimate edition because other versions were released after that one), one of the DVD's special features allows you to see how long it took to film an action sequence. This feature is succinctly called a "Multi-Angle Presentation of the Dailies from the Helicopter Acquisition Sequence, with subtitles for shooting dates and locations." By watching this special feature, you realize that shots filmed on 11/9/1990 cut to shots from 11/12/1990, then to shots from 2/14/1991, then to 11/13/1991, then to 3/14/1991, and so on, leaping around the calendar. Although this sequence may have taken many months to shoot, it plays out on-screen in a matter of a few minutes.

Each of those individual shots likely took many hours or even days to set up. After those lengthy setups, each shot probably took hours or minutes to film. And in the final edit, each shot lasts a couple of seconds or less. So as you can see, screen time is often not even remotely representative of the time spent setting up and shooting.

THE LINGO

Setup: On set, each shot that requires a new arrangement of lighting, props, or other elements is called a new "setup."

Example: "We shot 12 setups today."

Although action setups like those in *Terminator 2* are particularly complicated and thus take especially long to set up and shoot, the same idea is likely to be true on your film set to some degree. You too will likely spend far more time setting up than actually shooting. It is not uncommon for the actual shooting of the film to be the quickest part of the day. This is why so many actors demand nice trailers and why many people on set take up habits such as smoking, playing Sudoku, or lurking around the craft service table. This is also why most movies take between a few weeks and few years to shoot, but end up between 75 minutes and 3 hours in their final running times.

Key Points

- There is little correlation between screen time and shooting time.
- Just because movies are glamorous or exciting on-screen does not mean the set was.
- A shot that plays out on-screen in a matter of seconds takes much longer to set up.
- Filmmaking involves far more time getting ready to shoot than time actually shooting.

Fuck-Up #44

"I Need to Take My Time to Work"

Why the clock must always be ticking and how to cope

"You don't know what directing is until the sun is setting and you've got to get five shots and you're only going to get two."[3]

—David Fincher

The Fuck-Up...

Many new directors think it is their job to make sure everything is perfect, regardless of how long it takes. They're wrong.

Filmmaking, like life, involves a lot of compromises. Knowing how to make the compromises that will get the most out of the clock and therefore will benefit your film the greatest is one of the best traits any capable filmmaker must learn.

How to Do It Right...

Those new to film sets are often shocked not just by the lack of excitement, but also by the constant state of clock awareness and the anxiety it seems to be causing. Hearing the 1st assistant director (a.k.a. "1st A.D.") screaming about the time may seem unpleasant to outsiders, but this behavior seems routine to anyone who has spent some time on sets (for more on A.D.s and why they're screaming, read *Fuck-Up #36: "The Assistant Director Is the Director's Assistant"*). In filmmaking, no matter how much money is being spent, a leisurely pace is rarely affordable.

"Hurry up and wait" is a phrase you'll hear often on sets—meaning people are always rushing to get things ready, then after they are done panicking and are in fact finally ready, they have to wait because the set isn't ready for them. However, that does not mean the urgency was unnecessary. In film, it is crucial to be ready and waiting before you're needed. Time is of the essence, and if you're not ready and waiting, that means you run the risk of others waiting on you. Many assistant directors are very fond of the expression "Set waits on nothing. Everything waits on set." This means that your cast and crew should always be waiting for the set to be ready for them so that you never risk the opposite—having the set ready but waiting on the crew. A well-run set will absolutely have bored-looking people waiting for their moment. Otherwise, you run the risk of a lot of people standing around wasting expensive time because one person is not ready. So be bored, but be ready. Hurry up and wait.

Although time is always of the essence, it is not always time for any one particular crew or cast member to perform his or her particular job function—hence the reason there are so many people on set apparently doing nothing at any one time. However, when the moment strikes, a crew member's ability to be at the ready to do his job effectively, proficiently, and in a timely manner is absolutely crucial.

Planning ahead is even more crucial. If the cast and crew have just spent 20 minutes waiting for a lighting setup only to find out that now they must wait for a piece of wardrobe to be stitched up, the wardrobe person had better not have been one of those bored-looking people during that 20-minute lighting setup. The more your crew is able to stay several steps ahead of what is being shot, the better off everyone will be. This is why shooting schedules, shot lists, storyboards, lighting plans, and any other form of early planning you're capable of putting together are all so helpful. Your preparation will make possible the preparation of all those people who are there to help make your movie happen. Although, yes, the plan may change, a plan that is ever adapting will do you much greater good than no plan at all.

Key Points

- Time management is a key skill for any capable filmmaker to learn.
- Time is money.
- No matter what, the clock will always be ticking.
- "Hurry up and wait" is a good thing.
- Your crew should always stay several steps ahead of the set.
- The assistant directors are in charge of the schedule and keeping everyone informed as to its changes.
- Good planning will allow your crew to stay on top of things, even when the plan changes.

Fuck-Up #45

"Everyone Should Do What Needs to Be Done"

The importance of delegating responsibilities

"Delegating means letting others become the experts and hence the best."[4]
—Timothy Firnstahl

The Fuck-Up...

Many people who are new to film shoots are surprised by how specifically tasks are assigned to certain people and how often those people will not allow someone who is not in their department to help them out. This can be especially confusing and frustrating when the entire set is waiting for someone from the art department to make her way over to move a chair an inch to the right. However, there is method to the madness.

How to Do It Right...

The rules are that only the art department can touch the props, only the electric department can touch the lights, only the camera department can touch the camera, and so on. Why?

133

- **Expertise:** Sure, you might be able to move a light, but the electricians will have a better understanding of how to do it properly and safely, where they can move the power, and what the light should be doing. There is a plan, and if just anyone starts moving things, there will be confusion as to why and how the plan changed.
- **Sufficient staffing:** When certain people worry about certain things, it ensures that everything is getting worried about sufficiently. This is exactly what you want. If one person is worrying about catering, lighting, props, and wardrobe, he is likely to neglect some of those areas while being consumed with others. However, by allowing several people to focus on specific elements, they can give those details the type of time and attention they deserve.
- **Whose job is it anyway?:** When crew members have very specific responsibilities, you always know who to turn to in any situation to get something done. Time on set is far too valuable to spend it figuring out who should take care of something.
- **Job security:** Because you must allow only people within certain departments to do certain jobs, you have to hire enough people in every department to do those tasks. In other words, you have to hire more people.

As with many rules in filmmaking, depending on the circumstances, they should be broken. Many smaller productions will take an "everyone chips in mentality," and this can be an effective way of filmmaking. Having a small crew in which everyone pitches in to get done whatever is needed can be a great way to make a movie. In fact, these sets are often able to move at a faster pace by keeping the work small and contained. However, they run the risk of being understaffed, being overstressed, or not having anyone sufficiently qualified to perform certain specific tasks.

Decide what approach works effectively for your movie and make sure you have people who are on board with the crew style you want. If you want a set where everyone is allowed to cross "departmental lines" and chip in, hire a crew that will go along with that style of filmmaking. And if you want to have a set with very specific delegation of responsibilities to keep things clear, likewise, make sure your crew members are prepared to do their jobs well while not stepping on anyone else's proverbial toes.

Key Points

- Those working on set are given very specific delegation as to who is responsible for what.
- It is important to delegate responsibilities to not overwhelm any one individual.
- Clearly specifying who does what ensures that the job is done with expertise, is sufficiently staffed, and identifies whose responsibility it is.
- Some sets may want to take more of an "everyone chips in mentality."
- Hire a crew that is on board with the style of filmmaking you want.

Fuck-Up #46

"We Don't Need a Call Sheet"

Why this piece of paper is so damn important

"All great work is preparing yourself for the accident to happen."[5]

—Sidney Lumet

The Fuck-Up...

Filmmaking can involve a lot of paperwork, but despite its annoyance, some paperwork is actually very helpful and should not be skipped. A call sheet is a perfect example of one little piece of paperwork that can make or break your production.

How to Do It Right...

Call sheets are given out to the entire cast and crew so that they have the necessary information for the upcoming shooting day's work. A well-made call sheet contains a plethora of information that will answer a great deal of questions people may have regarding upcoming work. As you know, keeping your cast and crew well informed on what is coming up is crucial to a well-run set.

The call sheet includes information on who does what job, how to reach them, what scenes will be shot and in what order, who will be needed and at what time, how to get there, who will drive the vehicles, and so on. Call sheets come in many variations, and you should feel free to tailor your document to make the information that is most important to your shoot as easily accessible as possible. A couple of good call sheet samples you can use to get started are available online at filmmakerfups.com.

The call sheet contains so much valuable information that the best way to discuss it is to examine one. The two pages shown in Figures 46.1 and 46.2 are the front and back of a sample call sheet for a fake movie titled *Fake Movie*. Call sheets can be one- or two-sided documents. The sample call sheet shown here is a two-sided version. The actual document would be printed one page front and back, to make it easy to carry. Study it thoroughly to get a sense of the type of information a call sheet can provide (there are also some joke names in there to further entice you to study closely).

Making the daily call sheet is the responsibility of the 2nd assistant director, who as you may have guessed, is the number two person in the A.D. department. The 2nd A.D. will make drafts of the call sheet, which will need to be approved by the 1st A.D. and the line producer or production manager before being distributed to the crew daily.

Date: Wed., 7/20/2020								Day: 10 of 30

FAKE MOVIE

Prod Co.: Mediocre I

Director: Simon Sez
Writer: Oliver Clothesoff
Producer: I.P. Freely
UPM: Jacques Strap
Line Producer: Anita
1st AD: Sevmour Butz
2nd AD: Homer Sexual

BREAKFAST@9:30A. LUNCH@3:30P

PRODUCTION CALL: 9:00A
CREW CALL: 10:00A
SHOOTING CALL: 11:30A

SUNRISE: 6:04A
SUNSET: 7:57P
TWILIGHT: 7:28P
TEMP: 85°

WEATHER
Partly cloudy
High of 85° and low of 68°
Wind SWS

Set Cell Phones: Office 555-123-4567, 2nd AD 555-765-3210

SET-UPS	SCENE #	SET/DESCRIPTION	PAGES	CAST	D/N	LOCATION(S)
Tuesday, August 14, 2007						
# of shot 7	SC: 2	EXT. BAR *Guy walks out of bar.*	1	1	D2	SC 2 & SC 3: McGoldberg's Bar 815 Main St.
# of shots 1	SC: 3	EXT. STREET *Guy walks down street, meets Other Guy.*	1	1,3	N3	SC 1: McSomething Bara 217 Spooner Drive.
		<<<COMPANY MOVE!>>>				
# of shots 3	SC: 1	INT. BAR *Guy walks into a bar.*	1	1,2	D7	SC 4: The Place We Do Not Speak Of 216 Spooner Drive
# of shots 8	SC: 4	INT. ROOM *Guy and Other Guy go into a room.*	1	1,3	N1	
		TOTAL PAGES:	4			Truck, van and production parking: Paschal Middle School 200 Unquowa Rd

CAST INFO

CAST	SWF	#	CHARACTER	P/U	BLOCK	HMU	SET CALL	TRANSPORTATION
Mike Rotch	W	1	*Guy*	9:00A	10:00A	10:30A	11:30A	Teamster 1 Pickup
Alan Smithee	W	2	*Girl*	SR	2:00P	2:30P	3:30P	will self report
Wayne King	W	3	*Other Guy*	10:00A	10:00A	10:30A	11:30A	Teamster 2 Pickup

Personal vehicle parking:
In the river

BG, VEHICLES	COSTUME; H/MU	PROPS;SET DRESSING	DIRECTIONS TO SET
BACKGROUND	**COSTUME**	**PROPS**	Crew van will leave from The
SC: 2 - 12 Street Walkers	SC: 2 - Guy - rastafarian get-up, Other Guy t-shirt	SC: 2 - Chicken wings	Hotel that isn't as nice as where
SC: 1 - 5 Bar Patrons	SC: 3 - Guy - gorilla suit	SC. 1 - Beer and peanuts	we're sticking the actors @ 9:30A.
SC: 3 - 10 Parking Lot cars			

SFX; STUNTS	SPECIAL EQUIPMENT; LABOR	NOTES	CLOSET HOSPITAL
SPECIAL EFFECTS	**SPECIAL EQUIPMENT**	Mr. Rotch asks that nobdy	Our Merciless Lady
SC: 4 - Sun explodes	SC: 2- Jib	looks him in the eves.	123 Hope You're Insured Lane

Please be advised: **ALL SETS & HOLDING AREAS ARE NON-SMOKING.** Smoke only in the designated areas outside.
No forced calls or overtime without prior approval of Producer. All calls subject to change by Assistant Director.

ADVANCED SCHEDULE

Thursday, August 16th, 2007

SET-UPS	SCENE #	SET/DESCRIPTION	PAGES	CAST	D/N	LOCATION
# of shots 22	SC: 61	EXT. PARK *Dude wrestles a bear.*	3 1/8	1, 2	DFB8	**Stonecutter's Hall** **71 West 23rd St.** **New York, NY 10010**
# of shots 2	SC: 73	EXT. PARK *Bear gets final revenge on dude.*	1/8	1	N7	
		TOTAL PAGES:	3 1/2			

Friday, August 17th, 2007

SET-UPS	SCENE #	SET/DESCRIPTION	PAGES	CAST	D/N	LOCATION
# of shots 2	SC: 75	EXT. PARK *Guy gets attacked by Gary Busey, again.*	3	1, 7	N7	**Secret (will tell you later)**
		TOTAL PAGES:	3			

1st AD: Seymoure Butz	UPM: Jacques Strap
SEE BACK FOR INDIVIDUAL CALL TIMES	

Figure 46.1 *Sample call sheet: front.*

FAKE MOVIE   CALL SHEET BACK

Crew Call: 10:00A

Position	Name	Call	Out	TELEPHONE
Director	Simon Sez	10:00A		
Producer	I.P. Freely	O/C		
PRODUCTION				
UPM	Jacques Strap	9:00A		555-555-5555
Line Producer	Anita Bath	9:00A		555-555-5556
Prod. Acct.	Eura Snotball	O/C		555-555-5557
AD DEPARTMENT				
1st AD	Seymour Butz	10:00A		555-555-5555
2nd AD	Homer Sexual	10:00A		555-555-5556
2nd 2nd AD	Ollie Tabooger	10:00A		555-555-5557
Key PA	Ahmed Adoodie	9:00A		555-555-5558
Set PA	Oliver Klozoff	9:00A		555-555-5560
Set PA	Ura Snotball	9:00A		555-555-5561
Set Intern	Ima Hobbit	9:00A		555-555-5562
CAMERA				
D.P.	U. Snowit	10:00A		555-555-5563
1st A.C.	Anna Nymous	10:00A		555-555-5564
2nd A.C.	Ivana Snack	10:00A		555-555-5565
Loader	Holden Mcgroin	10:00A		555-555-5566
ART DEPARTMENT				
Prod. Designer	Ben Dover	10:00A		555-555-5563
Art Director	Eileen Dover	10:00A		555-555-5564
Props Master	Gina Tonic	10:00A		555-555-5565
Set Dresser	Chris Mass	10:00A		555-555-5566
CATERING/CRAFT SERVICES				
Caterer	Mac Arony	9:00A		555-555-5566
Chef	Dewey Decimal	9:00A		555-555-5567
ADDITIONAL LABOR				
Steadicam	Phil McCracken	O/C		555-555-5569
Crane Op.	Myra Placemen	O/C		555-555-5570
EDITORIAL				
Editor	Anita Cab	N/A		
Asst. Editor	Oliver Klozoff	N/A		555-555-5570
ELECTRIC DEPARTMENT				
Gaffer	Yuri Khant	10:00A		555-555-5670
Best Boy Elec.	Harry Nuckles	10:00A		555-555-5770
Swing	Harry Balzagna	10:00A		555-555-5870

Position	Name	Call	Out	TELEPHONE
GRIP DEPARTMENT				
Key Grip	Safanda Cox	10:00A		555-555-5570
Best Boy Grip	Dan Druff	10:00A		555-555-5571
2nd Grip	Robin Banks	10:00A		555-555-5572
WARDROBE DEPARTMENT				
Costume Designer	Phil McCrevis	10:00A		555-555-5571
Asst. Costume	Clyde Torres	10:00A		555-555-5572
Wardrobe Intern	Mary Huff	10:00A		555-555-5573
MAKE-UP & HAIR				
Key HMU	Annie Daynow	10:00A		555-555-5573
HMU Stylist	Terry Bull	10:00A		555-555-5574
MUSIC				
Composer	Helen Beck	N/A		555-555-5575
STUNTS				
Stunt Coordinator	Mabulsa Ritchie	O/C		555-555-5575
PUBLICITY				
Videographer/EPK	Ivanna Tinkle	N/A		555-555-5573
SCRIPT				
Script Supervisor	Justin Thyme	10:00A		555-555-5572
SOUND				
Sound Mixer	Pat McGroin	10:00A		555-555-5571
Boom Operator	Buck Naked			555-555-5572
CASTING				
Casting Director	Sal Monella	N/A		555-555-5573
Casting Assoc.	Flow Ryder	N/A		555-555-5574
Extras Casting	Lou Pole	N/A		555-555-5575
LOCATIONS				
Locations Mgr	Ura Snotball	10:00A		555-555-5578
Locations Asst.	Dixie Normus	10:00A		555-555-5579
TRANSPORTATION				
15 Pass Driver	Nancy Gosule			555-555-5579
Unit Truck Driver	John Robinson			555-555-5580
G&E Truck Driver	Sergio Q.			555-555-5581
Art Cube Driver	Will Lockwood			555-555-5582
Talent Vehicle	Eric Lord			555-555-5583
Talent Vehicle	Peter Tulba			555-555-5584

All Changes to Callsheet Information, Contact 2nd AD Homer Sexual 555-765-3210

Figure 46.2 *Sample call sheet: back.*

Another common mistake smaller movies make is asking the 1st A.D. to make the call sheets during production if there is no 2nd A.D. This is a *tremendous* fuck-up. Making the call sheet involves a good chunk of time sitting in front of a computer, and any time the 1st A.D. spends away from the set likely means they aren't managing the set and thus the on-set work is suffering. Hence, the 1st A.D. is pretty much the worst choice possible to make the call sheets. If a film doesn't have a 2nd A.D., someone in the production department, such as a production coordinator, should make the daily call sheets.

Most crew members keep their call sheets close at all times because they contain a plethora of helpful information. And so should you.

Key Points

- Call sheets are crucial.
- Call sheets are given out to the cast and crew daily.
- Call sheets inform individuals as to daily plans, what's being shot, when it's being shot, when they'll be needed, where they'll be needed, where to park, how to contact people, what people's names are, and much, much more.
- Making the call sheet is the 2nd A.D.'s job on most sets.
- If you're working on a film set, you should have a copy of the call sheet on you at all times.

Fuck-Up #47

"I'll Start with My Close-Ups"

How to organize your shots like a pro

"The secret of all victory lies in the organization of the non-obvious."[6]
—Marcus Aurelius, Roman emperor

The Fuck-Up...

If you were designing a building, one of your first steps would be to outline it to make sure it fit on the plot of land. After you had that broad outline, you would work your way in, gradually getting to smaller and smaller details: what the lobby will look like, how big the rooms can be, right down to where to put the electrical sockets. It is unlikely that you would start with the electrical sockets and work your way out from there, and simply pray that when you got to the end, the building would somehow all fit on the lot.

The same goes for your movie. Worrying about the big stuff before the smaller details ensures that when you're done, everything fits.

How to Do It Right…

On professional film sets, starting with your widest shot (also called your "master shot") and then working your way into closer "coverage" is a well-established routine. This is done for several reasons:

- It allows you to work out the scene in general before getting committed to the smaller details.
- It's the most time-efficient manner for lighting. And saving lighting time is a huge part of effective time management.
- It covers your ass. Because your master shot shows everything, should any other shots not work out or not get filmed at all, you still have the scene shot in its entirety. Like editors say, "When in doubt, you can always cut to the master."

> **THE LINGO**
>
> **Master shot:** A shot covering the entire scene and all on-screen characters.
>
> **Coverage:** Additional shots to augment that master shot. It is from the master shot and coverage that the editor builds the scene.
>
> Example: "Our coverage consisted of a master shot, a two-shot, singles, and close-ups for each character; an insert on an important prop; and a few cutaways."

If you start with your widest shot, you'll have established the look of the scene and have a sense of what your closer shots should look like. However, if you start with your close-ups, you still have no idea what the rest of the space should look like and will likely spend more time scrambling to work this out later.

So how can you best organize your shots? The answer (much like scheduling your whole movie) is to forget about chronology and organize for efficiency. Let's consider a simple scene for an example. This one involves a guy and a girl sitting at a table talking:

                    GUY

                     Hi

                    GIRL

                   Hello

                    GUY

                How are you?

                    GIRL

                   Good

First, you'll start with your master shot, where you can see the entire scene, including all its characters (in this case, "Guy" and "Girl"). This will help you work out the scene as a whole before getting into the details.

After you've done the master shot of the scene, you can go in for closer coverage. You'll want to continue to organize your shots for efficiency. Let's say that the early morning light is better for the "Girl" character, so you'd like to shoot her before the guy, even though the guy speaks first (see, we're out of movie order already). After you finesse the lighting, hair, makeup, and wardrobe so all is just perfect for her, you are going to shoot all her stuff together. Even though the scene goes back and forth— Guy talks, Girl talks, Guy talks, Girl talks—you will want to shoot together all the shots in which the Girl will be seen, while you're ready for her, rather than going back and forth.

> **THE LINGO**
>
> **Turnaround:** Going from shooting in one direction to another.
>
> Example: "We're going to shoot a new side of the room now, so we'll have a 60-minute turnaround for lighting and art."

Film every shot looking at one character in one direction before turning around. "Turning around" means looking a new direction you have not shot yet, which means preparing an entire new area with art direction, set dressing, lighting, and so on. Thus, you see why it makes sense to shoot together absolutely everything in one direction. Turning around and then back to an area you've already shot is a surefire sign of a rookie director who does not understand how a film set should operate. Try your best to group together all your coverage looking one way. This may require careful shot listing and planning, but after you've mastered the concept, it will undoubtedly come naturally to you and make your production a better one.

Going back to our simple scene for a moment, imagine the ludicrousness of taking 40 minutes to set up a shot for the Guy to say "Hi," then another 40 minutes to set up a shot for the Girl to say "Hello," and then taking another 40 minutes to re-create the Guy's shot again, for him to now say his second line, "How are you?" You can begin to imagine that when you apply this approach to a more complicated scene, things rapidly become exponentially harder and more time consuming. Thus, grouping shots for efficiency is crucial.

If you do not have a firm grasp on how to group shots for efficient shooting, that's okay. As always, there are people whose job it is to help. Your director of photography and 1st A.D. should be the first people you speak with when discussing in what order to accomplish your shots. Your director of photography will no doubt be more than happy to tell you the sequence of shots that would be the most efficient for her to shoot. However, keep in mind that while the D.P. is responsible for the look, lighting, and camera work, there is much she is not responsible for and thus may not be considering when it comes to scheduling for efficiency.

Grouping for lighting is the best way to approach scheduling your shot list the overwhelming majority of the time—but not always. D.P.s may neglect to think about certain things that also come into play when scheduling your shots, such as time spent resetting makeup, wardrobe, props, or hair changes that also need to be considered. If a scene involves a character getting bloody, it would be easier to group together all the stuff without blood on the actor and all the stuff with blood, respectively. This is more efficient than constantly covering the actor in blood, washing her off, and then putting her back in the blood bucket. So make your A.D. and D.P. the first stops in determining your shot schedule, and as always, keep in mind the specific demands of a scene and consult with other departments to find out what order of shooting would make things most efficient overall.

And as with any good rule, at times you should ignore it. For emotional scenes, some directors insist on shooting close-ups first out of fear that the actors will be too worn out to perform well later. If circumstances make ignoring the rules of efficient shooting necessary, then so be it. Use your best judgment; it's important that you get it done but also done well.

Key Points

- Start with your widest shots and then work your way in to closer shots.
- Organize your shots for efficiency, not chronology.
- Shoot everything looking in one direction before looking in another direction to minimize "turning around."
- Look for ways to minimize repeating work by grouping shots that will require the same elements.
- Consult with your 1st A.D. and director of photography on how to most efficiently organize your shots.
- As with any rules, ignore efficient shot listing when necessary.

Fuck-Up #48

"I Need More/Less Coverage"

How to know when you've got it and when you don't

"The secret to survivin' is knowin' what to throw away and knowin' what to keep."[7]
—Kenny Rogers, "The Gambler"

The Fuck-Up…

Knowing exactly how your final movie will come together, while you're still shooting it, is nearly impossible. So it can be difficult to be sure what shots you will or will not need. Not having the correct shots to piece together a scene is a classic first-time filmmaker mistake—as is wasting a lot of time getting shots you'll never use.

How to Do It Right…

THERE ARE *INFINITE* WAYS TO SHOOT ANY SCENE.

Frequently, when people use the word "infinite," they do not mean it literally. (And "literally" is another word people often misuse. Someone once told me "You scared me so bad, I literally shit my pants." When I asked him to see his pants, he had to confess he meant the statement "figuratively," not literally.) In this case, I want it to be clear that I literally mean exactly what I am saying: there are *infinite* ways to shoot any scene.

There is no limit to the number of theoretical possibilities of how to shoot any given scene. Positioning the camera an extra inch to the left, right, up, or down changes the shot. It can alter the perspective, the feel, perhaps even the significance of the shot. How you move the camera, how quickly it makes that motion, how you zoom, what lens you use—all these factors affect your work. The shot you ultimately choose will be plucked from the infinite. And from those infinite possibilities, there is no "right choice." It is a matter of aesthetics and taste. However, getting good "coverage" with your shots will ultimately prove crucial in ensuring you can assemble a quality scene in the edit.

I like to think of the term "coverage" as having a double meaning: to cover the scene and to cover your ass. This means getting enough angles and takes that you can actually put together a quality scene, with options, and edit around anything that might come to need editing around. Want to lose a line that isn't working? Need to hide a continuity error? Trying to remove an entire character from your film? Well, you will need the proper coverage to make these editorial changes possible.

The way to mentally approach coverage is to always be editing in your mind's eye. Ask yourself:

- What will each shot cut to and from?
- Have your shots covered all the necessary action?
- Do you know when you want to cut in tighter from a wider shot? Or wider from a tight?

- Will the shots and their variety keep the scene as visually interesting as you'd like?
- Do you need to show inserts on details?
- Do you need to have cutaways to help piece the scene together?
- At any given moment, what character or action do you want the audience's attention on?

If you have not yet decided the answer to any of these questions or simply are not sure, your concern should be whether you have options. Do you have a few good choices as to what shot you could cut to and from? Have you covered enough dialogue in wider and tighter coverage to choose later when you will cut in? Do you have cutaways just in case you need them? Do you have the variations in performance that will allow you to decide what to go with later?

When you set out to make a movie, you will, in fact, make three different movies: the movie you write, the movie you shoot, and the movie you edit. Just as you need to have enough written to give yourself something to shoot, you need to have enough shot to give yourself something to edit. Unless you have an incredibly clear vision of your edit, give yourself options. You may not even know what you will need until months later, when you're trying to change a scene or fix an unexpected problem in the edit long after the cameras have stopped rolling.

Frequently, the greater challenge is in knowing what you do not need. Because directing is, in part, about time management, knowing what you can do without is incredibly important. Being able to picture how a shot fits into a scene is like imagining how a tree fits into the forest, and it must be done. You might need to re-imagine the entire forest on the fly, so be ready. It's important to have enough coverage to "cover" your scene and your ass. However, getting too much coverage can prevent you from completing the day's work. And no matter how good what you have is, an incomplete scene is useless.

A good director of photography and/or script supervisor can help advise on the type of coverage a particular scene may require. Many other people on set will also be happy to give their opinions on what shots they think are or are not needed. However, a word of warning: some people on set like to say things such as "They don't really need this shot." Unless those people are in a very clear position to know how the scene is envisioned and how it will be edited, they don't know what they're talking about. Furthermore, if they do not clearly know every take you have already accomplished to the degree where they can tell you how each line was read in each of those takes, those people do not know what the scene is lacking. Only the director has the job of knowing when he has what he truly needs and when he does not. Ignoring those who do not know what they are talking about is just as important as listening to those who do.

Key Points

- There are infinite ways to shoot any scene.
- Good coverage means you have options for every moment when it comes time to edit the scene.
- Imagine your edit when thinking about coverage.
- Give yourself options in the edit. You may not even know what options you need until it's too late to get them.
- Your director of photography and script supervisor can help you determine what coverage is necessary.
- Be wary of uninformed people telling you what shots you do or do not need.
- Only the director is ultimately responsible for knowing what he has and what he needs.

Fuck-Up #49

"I Know What Film Sets Should Be Like"

Why your expectations may be mistaken

"A good director's not sure when he gets on the set what he's going to do."[8]
—Elia Kazan

The Fuck-Up…

There is no truly "typical day on set." Part of what makes filmmaking such an amazing vocation is that every day is unique. One day you could be filming a famous actor in an exotic paradise, on another day you could be shooting in a zero-gravity airplane plummeting at breakneck speeds toward the earth, and on yet another day you might be standing in a pile of manure trying to get a horse to act on cue. Any location, any activity, and all types of people may be on a film set depending on any movie's particular needs on a particular day.

Film sets, like film technology, are always changing, and every project is unique. It is a mistake to think of any set as "typical." Nevertheless, in case you have never been on a film set before, it's helpful to get a general sense of what you *may* be in for.

How to Do It Right...

Here's a general understanding of what a (for lack of a better word) "typical" day on set might be like:

- At an ungodly hour that no normal person would go to work (either incredibly early or late), members of the production department arrive EVEN BEFORE THE CREW CALL TIME. A representative of the production department and helpful P.A.s make sure that the location has access, that the office is set up, and that breakfast is ready when the crew arrives.

- The production department immediately begins dealing with that day's set of problems. Here are just a few of the infinite possibilities that have actually occurred: the director's car is lost, the unit production truck ran into a ditch, some idiot stole the fake prop money, an actor isn't happy with his hair person, the director decided he wants an unscheduled crane immediately, the teamsters union is protesting out front, or the fire department is shaking down the producers for money.

- At a slightly later hour (that still seems painfully early or late), it's the crew's call time. The crew shows up, and breakfast is ready for them (the first meal is called "breakfast" even if the work is starting at midnight).

- Later, the 1st A.D., director, actors, and D.P. start to trickle in. The P.A.s call out each arrival over walkie-talkies. This helps inform everyone in one large stroke.

- General pleasantries and hellos are exchanged, followed by a quick bite, with the goal of getting to blocking as soon as possible because a lot of work is waiting and the 1st A.D. is already panicking because the day almost always starts with some sort of setback.

- The director and actors "block the scene," figuring out the general action of the scene: who's going to go where and when they are going to go there. This isn't a rehearsal in the sense that it is not so much about the performance as it is a reference to plan the shooting strategy and for the crew to see the

THE LINGO

Blocking: Figuring out the general action of a scene, where the actors will be, and what types of movements they'll make. This gives the crew an idea of what to expect for the scene so they can set up and plan accordingly.

Example: Conventional work chronology is to first, block; second, light; then third, shoot.

scene and know what to plan for. It's fine to save the emotions of a performance for when it matters and just sort of go through the motions here.

- After the actors and director have worked out the blocking, the department heads come in and watch a blocking rehearsal. This way, the D.P. gets a sense of what to shoot, the gaffer knows what to light, the sound mixer knows what to mic, the art director knows what will be seen on camera, and so on.

- After the crew see what they need to know to do their respective jobs, the actors are whisked off to the "works" (meaning hair, makeup, and wardrobe).

- Meanwhile, the director, D.P., and 1st A.D. figure out how they want to shoot the scene and in what order those shots will go (if they haven't figured this out previously).

- The 1st A.D. informs all the necessary crew people of the game plan (or changes to the game plan they already knew about).

- The D.P. talks to his gaffer and key grip about their own game plan, and the crew begins lighting and prepping the set (the art department was working ahead of the shooting crew, so the set was likely mostly built, dressed, and ready before the blocking).

- When the first shot is set up and the necessary actors are prepared, the 1st A.D. calls out "first shot is up" (meaning ready). This process may all sound simple, but it can be hours into the day before the first shot is actually being shot.

- The actors come back to set finished with hair, makeup, and wardrobe. They get ready for either a rehearsal or the first shot. The 1st A.D. calls out all these steps as she dutifully manages the set.

- Right before the take, "last looks" are called for, and the hair, makeup, and wardrobe people run in to tinker with the actors one last time right before the shot.

> **THE LINGO**
>
> **Last looks:** When hair, makeup, and wardrobe staff get one more opportunity to put the final touches on the actors right before the camera rolls.

- The 1st A.D. calls for "quiet." The P.A.s echo the 1st A.D., repeating "quiet" to let everyone know it's that time. The 1st A.D. says "roll sound," and the sound mixer responds "speed," meaning he is recording. Next is "roll camera," and the camera operator says "mark it" when he's recording and ready for the slate. The slate is clapped and then removed, and the camera operator says "camera set" to let everyone know he is ready, and then "action!"

- Then the actors perform the scene (which is, of course, the part everyone wants to see and also the part that often takes up the least actual time).

- The director calls "cut," and everyone resets whatever needs resetting to get ready for another take of the same thing.

- Perhaps at this point the director gives the actors some notes, and they get ready to do the scene again.
- The process is repeated: last lookers come in, last lookers run out, "Quiet... rolling... speed... slate... action... cut."
- After that take, the director might give more notes, decide to try a different variation, or ask for a "safety," which is really just another way of saying "I want another option."
- When everyone is happy with that shot, the director says "print" on the takes she likes. The gate is checked (if shooting on film), which means the 1st A.C. looks into the camera to make sure there are no stray particles of film (called "hairs"). If the gate is clean, the 1st A.C. calls out "good gate," and everyone begins to get ready for the next shot.
- Setting up the next shot can take awhile, so the actors might be whisked back off set to their trailer or a place they can hang out. The "2nd team" (stand-ins) comes in to stand in the actors' places as the crew gets ready for the next "setup."
- Props are moved as needed and the new shot is lit and set up.
- A little time goes by (hopefully, just a little), and the next shot is ready. The actors come back out, more "last looks," and the shooting process is repeated. "Quiet... rolling... speed... slate... action... cut." The same scene can be done again and again for different takes and different angles (master shots, two-shots, medium shots, close-ups, the other actor's medium shot, the other actor's close-up, the other actor's shots, inserts, and so on).
- After all the shots for the scene are accomplished, the scene is done in its entirety. Or so you thought. Then the sound person reminds you that you need room tone. So everyone holds really still for 30–60 seconds so that they can record the sound of the room.

> **THE LINGO**
>
> **Room tone:** The sound a location naturally makes. It is recorded to use as filler in the soundtrack during editing.

- Now that the scene is really done, the setup can be torn down. Meanwhile, it is on to the next scene. This means you go back to blocking.
- It's back to block, then light, then shoot—oh, but wait; look at the time. "That's lunch everybody!" To avoid paying penalties for cutting into everyone's lunch (a meal break is generally guaranteed at least every six hours), work will have to wait until after the cast and crew eat.
- The crew breaks for lunch for an allotted amount of time (usually 30 minutes or an hour), but that time does not start being counted until the LAST crew member has his food. This guarantees everyone gets a full lunch break for the promised amount of time.
- When the last crew member has his food, "last man" (meaning the last person to get his food) is called out. And this announcement tells everyone when the crew will be "back in" (getting

back to work). So someone might yell out something like "Last man at 12:34; we're back in at 1:04."

- After lunch, you pick up where you left off: block, light, shoot, hopefully keeping up a good pace, completing all the work that was scheduled for today, or else it will be "owed." This means you'll have to figure out where, in the already tight schedule, you can do what you didn't accomplish today.

- During any down time, the director answers the numerous questions a director is required to answer (such as picking wardrobe for the next day or locations for the next week, discussing a character with an actor, figuring out how to rework a scene because the location/actor/mariachi band fell through).

- Look at the time already: the last shot is up. The 1st A.D. calls out "the martini is up" (the last shot is called the "martini" because the next shot will be in a glass. Get it?) The crew members attempt to restrain their excitement at almost ending a long day, but you can feel it in the room anyway.

- After the last shot of the day, the actors get out of wardrobe and makeup and sign out (SAG loves paperwork).

- Meanwhile, the crew is still busy either taking down the lights and sets from today's work or setting up the lights and sets for the next day's work.

- The Director, D.P., editor, and whoever else is invited, go off to watch dailies from the previous days' work. They review the dailies, pat each other on the back, and discuss whether there is anything they would like to reshoot.

> **THE LINGO**
>
> **Dailies:** Scenes of previous days' work for review. The term refers more specifically to projects shot on film, in which the processed film was rushed over from the lab *daily*.

- Although everyone is already very drowsy from an excruciatingly long day, a few more questions and meetings are squeezed in before heading home for…

- Sleep (hopefully) and repeat tomorrow.

Key Points

- There is no real "typical day" on set.
- A general understanding of how sets function is helpful.
- There's a lot to do every day on set.

Fuck-Up #50

"We'll Fix It in Post"

Why this joke is dangerous

"Never put off till tomorrow what you can do today."[9]

—Thomas Jefferson

The Fuck-Up...

"Fix it in post" is an old joke often heard on film sets. Indeed, post-production is amazingly powerful and can be utilized to fix a lot of issues that may have arisen during shooting. However, assuming you'll be able to fix all your problems in post is a costly and often ignorant assumption.

Perhaps the worst part of the "fix it in post" mentality is that people with little understanding of how post-production works often suggest it. If you are a post-production expert and know what visual and sound elements can be corrected later, by all means you should utilize that expertise. Knowing what is best left to post can save a tremendous amount of valuable set time. And, if you don't have such expertise, you can rely on visual and audio post professionals to tell you what can be accomplished when that stage is reached. However, you should be very wary of people on set without this expertise uttering those well-meaning but dangerous words, "fix it in post," because you may find out far too late that they were wrong.

How to Do It Right...

Want to edit a character out of movie? How about change the sequence of events? Alter the look of a scene? Or add an element that wasn't even there when you shot? All of this and more are possible in post-production. And with careful planning, you can set yourself up to do truly incredible things in post—but not everything.

It is far easier to address issues on set, when you have the necessary actors, props, lighting, and other resources at your fingertips, than in post-production. When attempting to fix something in post, directors more often than not end up kicking themselves for not having taken care of the problem while they had the chance to on set.

Let's say you're not happy with a performance. You can attempt to edit out the poor acting later, or you can address it on set and perhaps get something usable from your actor (or replace your actor with someone who will give you more to work with). If a special effect isn't quite working, if you fix it while shooting, you will know exactly what you have rather than gambling what it may or may not look like if you leave it to post. Or if your sound quality isn't so good, you can try to address the problem on set or spend a lot more money in what can be excruciating attempts to rebuild all the sound that should have been captured on set and still may never sound right.

These are just a few examples, but any post-production professional will likely tell you, if you can accomplish something on set rather than in post, you are likely to be far happier with the results. If you're unsure whether something can be fixed in post, always play it safe: assume it cannot be fixed later and fix it on set.

The issues that post-production can handle best are the ones you plan. In the digital age, it may be easy for a director to say, "Put a dinosaur here, here, and there." But in order for it to look good, it must be carefully planned for while shooting.

Key Points

- Post-production is amazingly powerful and can be used to change and "fix" a lot of the problems of a film.
- It takes expertise to know what can and cannot be fixed in post.
- It takes expertise to know what is required to fix something in post.
- Be wary of people who tell you something can be "fixed in post" if they do not have a thorough understanding of what you need and what it will take to accomplish that later.
- When in doubt, you are much better off fixing problems during shooting rather than in post-production.

Editing

Fuck-Up #51

"Anyone with a Computer Can Edit"

Why editing well takes a lot more than software

"Film editing is now something almost everyone can do at a simple level and enjoy it, but to take it to a higher level requires the same dedication and persistence that any art form does."[1]

—Walter Murch

The Fuck-Up...

Lots of people have editing software. Some computers even come with it already pre-installed. However, as with any job, having equipment does not make you the best person for the position. You can learn the basics of editing fairly easily, but it takes experience to develop the skills to actually do the job well.

Lots of people proclaim themselves editors because they own editing software (in the same way you can declare yourself a D.P. by buying a camera). Although having the right equipment is certainly crucial, there is a lot more to finding the right editor for your movie.

How to Do It Right...

Some editors have a god-like complex, and in the world of the film they are editing, they are right. Editors can change everything in the movie's universe with a few strokes of their almighty keyboard. They can mold an actor's performance, set the emotional pacing of the movie, alter the story, and influence what will live on in the eternity of a film and what will unceremoniously die on the cutting room floor.

An editor's simple decisions do not have simple influences on a movie and its performances. With a few clicks, the editor can take a reaction that was meant for a completely different line and use it any way she sees fit. So in this sense, yes, the editor is absolutely the puppet master of much of your movie's creative destiny. Whether the editor lets an actor sigh before he speaks can determine whether he seems sincere or conniving. A moment of eye contact lingering an extra beat can turn apathy into intrigue. Adding a pause for comic timing can be the difference between a line garnering a huge laugh and the sound of crickets filling the theater.

You need an editor who truly understands your movie, what it is you're going for, how the movie should feel, how she can contribute to that vision—and also one who has the technical skill set to accomplish it all. If you're making a comedy, your editor better have a great sense of comic timing. If it's a thriller, your editor needs to know how to build tension. The editor doesn't just put the pieces together; she helps mold and reform the story, the characters, and the pace.

An editor must be technically savvy. Nearly all professional film editing is now done on computers, and as you likely already know, computers almost always entail a fair amount of technical troubleshooting. Having an editor (or assistant editor) who's capable of handling the tech stuff can be as important as handling the creative stuff.

> **THE LINGO**
>
> **Assistant editor:** The person who handles many of the tasks required to edit a movie so as to leave the editor free to focus on the creative work. These tasks can include importing, synching, labeling, and organizing the footage as well as troubleshooting technical issues.

Remember that the film you write, the film you shoot, and the film you edit are three different movies. Your editor is going to have tremendous influence over that final draft of the film—the one that audiences will actually see. Thus, you must choose carefully who has this responsibility.

Key Points

- You should never hire an editor solely because she owns equipment.
- Learning to edit is easy; learning to edit well takes talent and experience.
- You must hire an editor who truly understands your movie.
- A good editor will make your movie vastly better.
- The editor has god-like control over the world of your film.

Fuck-Up #52

"You Don't Need to Watch ALL the Footage"

Why you should be familiar with every frame you shot

"First cuts are a bitch for a director.... You look at it and go,
'This is terrible. I hate it.'"[2]
—Richard Donner

The Fuck-Up...

In the early stages of editing, reviewing all your footage can seem rather time consuming and maybe even pointless, especially if you have a clear vision of what you want. However, what you want at the beginning of the process and what you want throughout the editing process is very likely to change. Only by knowing all your footage well will you know what changes are possible.

How to Do It Right...

Months after you start editing, you may find yourself working on a scene and think of a shot that you trashed from another scene that you could cheat in to help make this scene better. However, if you don't know your footage well, you will never appreciate all that is already at your fingertips. The better you know your footage, the better you can manipulate it to improve your movie.

> **THE LINGO**
>
> **Cheat:** In editing, to use a clip (the picture, sound, or both) in a completely different manner than it was originally intended for.

You should know your footage better than you know yourself. The more you and/or your editor know every frame, the better it can serve you and your movie. You never know what little snippet of a look, a line, or an accident you will be able to utilize. Thus, it's important to review all your footage at the beginning of editing and remind yourself of it periodically throughout the process.

After you have reviewed all your footage, you should start your first "assembly" with a similar approach. The assembly is the cut that will most resemble your movie's script. That means putting everything in, and in the order it was scripted. As happens when you review your footage, your assembly will likely involve a lot of things that will not survive all the way through to the final edit. You should include things you know do not work, the slow parts, the bad jokes, the awkward scenes, and so on. This cut may be painful to watch at times, but looking at everything together is a crucial tool for moving forward with your future cuts.

Until you can look at your movie as a whole, you don't even know what it is you have. Being able to get a sense of all that is in front of you will begin to generate ideas on how to rework it. Only then will you feel where your movie lags, where lines do not work, and where scenes can be re-ordered. Sure, the assembly will be too long and will drag at times, but think of it as a tool to create the product—not the product itself. And even if you have a very clear vision as to the bulk of your edit, the assembly is still a great means of seeing it all laid out for that small (but important) percentage of your movie you may not have already worked out in your head.

Keep in mind that no rule says anyone in the outside world ever has to see your assembly. It is a tool for you and your editor alone to use. Your assembly absolutely needs work; that's the point of it—to help make clear what future work will be necessary, which is possible only if you've seen everything.

Key Points

- The more you are familiar with all your footage, the better you can utilize it.
- Early on, you might not know what you need, but by knowing your footage well, you will know what is possible.
- The first cut of the film should most closely reflect the script and include everything—even the parts you know will get cut out later.
- Often you'll need to see the whole movie pieced together to understand where the problems lie.
- Nobody needs to see your first cut; it is a tool for you and your editor.

Fuck-Up #53

"Editing Shouldn't Hurt"

Why editing needs to be a painful process

"If you do not change direction, you may end up where you are heading."[3]

—Lao Tzu

The Fuck-Up…

By the time you reach the edit, you may have a strong vision of what your film should be. After all, you have been imagining it throughout writing, casting, pre-production, and shooting. However, you may also reach the edit and realize that much of what you've imagined and dreamt about simply is not working.

Perhaps the single element that you are most attached to in your movie somehow just can't be made to work. Well, much like in writing or in shooting, your vision must adapt to change for the greater good. Losing things that we love is always difficult, but it is also extremely necessary.

How to Do It Right…

Certain things you are passionately in love with simply will not survive your edit. As you first discovered way back in the script *Fuck-Ups*, much of filmmaking deals with coping with creative loss. In the screenwriting stage, we discussed how some of your favorite material may have been cut because it did not serve the overall movie or because of the limitations of your schedule and/or budget. During production, some fantastic stuff may have been cut due to time, budget, or an infinite number of other constraints. The same is true in the edit. Some things you love will not survive, and you will have to find a way to cope with that loss.

Dealing with the loss of elements you love can be an especially difficult thing for first-time filmmakers to come to grips with. Try to remind yourself that you are making a movie and that the film as a whole is more important than its individual parts. It is a communist-like mentality, but in the case of your movie, it is the correct mentality. Sure, you may have loved a joke or a line, but if it's not working, cut it.

Furthermore, sometimes it's necessary to cut something that *is* working. If a scene or the film itself is not working, trimming bits and pieces that may work fine by themselves can often help the overall movie. A long scene, even one packed with great moments, can still feel too long—if that is the case then trimming it can help the film work better. Frequently, some good moments will have to be lost for the greater good.

The most difficult parts to let go are those that we know were particularly challenging or expensive to accomplish. Far too many directors have uttered the words, "I can't cut that. Do you know how hard that shot was to get?" or "Do you know how expensive that was?" The reality is, your audience does not know *or care* how difficult or expensive something was to achieve. They only know whether or not your movie is working. So although I have empathy with your pain in cutting a shot that you, your crew, and perhaps your wallet bled for, if it is not serving your movie, it must be left behind. If it helps you to cope with the loss, know that perhaps you can save that idea for your next movie. Chances are, nobody will ever know you borrowed from yourself anyway.

Key Points

- Parting with an idea you love can be very difficult, but it is still necessary if doing so makes your movie better.
- Certain parts of your movie you are in love with will not survive to the final edit.
- Some things that may work great on their own will not work within the overall scene or film and must be cut.
- Even if something was difficult or expensive to shoot, it should not stay in your film unless it's making the movie better.

Fuck-Up #54

"Editing Will Take a Few Passes"

Why editing is re-editing...more than you think

"Nothing will work unless you do."[4]
—Maya Angelou

The Fuck-Up...

New filmmakers are quick to celebrate after completing a cut of their movie. They feel as though the finish line is in sight and they will soon have a masterpiece to show the world. Although finishing a cut of your film is a great feeling and an incredible accomplishment, you still have plenty of work ahead.

How to Do It Right...

After your assembly, you will, I hope, have many more rounds of editing. Always remember that each cut needs to be better than the last. This is another one of those suggestions that sounds obvious but is not always the case. Some editors simply can't resist the urge to tweak or try something differently or the power surge of cutting things out. Some of your changes may, in fact, make the movie worse. That's fine, as long as you realize this fact and take them back. The "undo" command can be an editor's best friend.

An important part of the editing process is trial and error and it should be utilized thoroughly. Let's say you're not sure which take is the best. The great thing about post-production unlike production, is that the clock is not likely to be ticking quite so intensely because there are not nearly as many people standing around whom you have to pay while they wait for a decision to be made. So, take the time to make alternate versions of edits that you can watch side by side to decide what's best. Trying different takes and different cutting points will quickly give you a sense of just how many different ways your movie can feel based on any individual cut. The cut is a powerful thing, and you should experiment with that power freely.

Often the only way to know if a cut is right is to feel it. Feeling a cut can be a very instinctive experience. If you don't believe me, try cutting two shots together at three different moments. I am willing to wager that some of those cuts will *feel* better than others. It is a difficult thing to articulate but a remarkable thing to experience. So do not be afraid of trial and error until the cut feels right.

Most likely your film will improve in part by getting progressively shorter, or "tighter" as we say. Because your assembly included everything your script had and then some, getting progressively shorter is the logical approach with each round of editing. You will take out parts that do not work. You will take out parts that just don't work quite as well as other parts. Very frequently, making things faster will make them better. You will get to the heart and soul of your movie. And you will trim every ounce of what appears to be fat.

Adjusting how images are juxtaposed will also help your movie evolve. Psychological studies on juxtaposition have demonstrated that we perceive an image's meaning based in part on its relation to other images. One common test involves showing test subjects the same picture of a person next to other varying images. Then the subject is asked what he thinks the person in the picture was feeling. When the person was shown next to a baby, the test subject frequently thought the person was feeling love. When the person was next to a house crushed by a tornado, the test subject thought the person was feeling sadness. And so on and so forth. The same picture with the same expression was perceived to be expressing different emotions depending on what it was put next to.

> **THE LINGO**
>
> **Juxtaposition:** The manner in which things are placed side by side. In the edit, how the sequencing of shots affects their meaning.

The same theory applies to editing. You must feel how your images service each other by which image you put next to which other images. The editor can take one shot of an actor's expression and completely change how the audience feels about it based on what other image it is juxtaposed with. Furthermore, the editor not only decides what images go where, but also controls the timing of these moments. Timing is just as crucial to the feel as juxtaposition.

Finally, although it is important to know when your movie still needs work, it is equally important to know when to stop. At a certain point, the "law of diminishing returns" may kick in, meaning that the film is getting better but by smaller and smaller amounts until the differences are inconsequential. Worse yet, at a point the work may begin to make your film worse, not better—and you may not be objective enough to appreciate this fact while doing so. My father, who is an engineer, put it another way when he explained to me a theory called "shooting the engineer." He said, "If allowed, an engineer will work on one invention forever, always thinking he can make it better. So at some point, you just have to shoot the guy in the head and take it from him." The same is true for your movie. Sure, you could continue editing it for the rest of your life. Chances are, when you watch your movie 60 years after completing it, you will still see something you'd like to improve. However, at some point, although it may not be perfect, it will come time to shoot the editor (metaphorically, I hope).

Key Points

- Editing takes numerous rounds of revisions.
- Cut sections that do not work—or do not work as well as the rest of your film.
- Trial and error is a wonderful tool to figure out what works best.
- Often you must intrinsically feel a cut to find the best edit.
- How images are sequenced and timed greatly changes their meaning and effect.
- Although a movie can always be tweaked further, at some point you simply have to stop editing and let go.

Fuck-Up #55

"This Cut Is Good Enough to Show"

The importance of first impressions with your film

"You never get a second chance to make a first impression."
—author unknown

The Fuck-Up...

While you are editing, people will often ask to see your movie even if it is still a work in progress. They'll tell you they "just want to see a little something" or "they know how to view a rough cut." However, if these people are important to your movie's future, showing an early cut without all the kinks worked out is very dangerous. No matter what anyone says, you get only one first impression.

How to Do It Right...

Nobody knows how to view a rough cut. When I say this, I really mean not a single soul on this planet—or for that matter, on any other planet. A lot of people will tell you that they "know how to view rough cuts." They will say this as a lure to get you to show them your movie before it is ready. They may even believe they really do possess this power. However, not editors, not directors, not your psychic—nobody knows "how to view a rough cut"—because it is impossible to watch with the level of objectivity that phrase implies.

It is basic human nature to make first impressions and to maintain them. No matter what state the film is in, opinions will be formed for better or for worse. Watching an incomplete movie still creates a movie-going experience. And once that experience—and first impression—has been made, it will never go away, regardless of how the movie changes later.

People can say, "Well, after you have the music in there and make some trims, I think it'll really...." But they have already had a movie-going experience that is valid unto itself and that experience is there forever. Furthermore, nobody, not even you, actually has the ability to know exactly what your final product will be. People can only judge the movie that you have made until this point. How can any viewers know what your next cut will involve? How score will help manipulate the emotion of the movie? How radically the color correction will affect the feel of your film? And if they cannot turn off those forward-thinking thoughts, how can they let go and enjoy the movie to begin with?

This is not to say that you should not show early cuts or that reactions to early cuts are inherently doomed. Outside feedback is crucial to your film's evolution into the best movie possible (we'll discuss that more in the next *Fuck-Up*). But you should be selective to whom you show early cuts. If there are people you'd like to impress, wait. If you stick by the rule of "every cut should be better than the last," showing early cuts means you are not putting your best foot forward. Think carefully about whose feedback is valuable and, more importantly, whose opinion matters to the future of your movie and your career. If it is someone such as a distributor that may affect your film's future, it is crucial to make your first impression as positive as possible. Yes, these people might promise to also watch an updated cut again later, but it will be nearly impossible for them to erase the opinion they've already formed of your movie. No matter how much objectivity is promised, it simply goes against human nature to change a first impression easily. Furthermore, a distributor might decide he is not interested based on an early cut and be unwilling to watch later cuts. And even worse yet, distributors know each other and often talk. Poor word of mouth may travel about your film before it's even finished, thus killing its chances at obtaining quality distribution based solely on an incomplete version of your film.

Key Points

- Nobody knows "how to view a rough cut" because it is impossible to watch with the level of objectivity that phrase implies.
- It is human nature to make first impressions, and it is difficult to erase those impressions regardless of how much the movie changes later.
- You should be selective to whom you show early cuts.
- Early cuts should be shown for feedback, but not to people whose opinion is important to the film's future (such as distributors).
- Showing early cuts to certain people may cause bad word of mouth early.

Fuck-Up #56

"I Don't Need Outside Feedback"

The importance of feedback: when to listen and when not to

"For I am not so enamoured of my own opinions that
I disregard what others may think of them."[5]
—Nicolaus Copernicus

The Fuck-Up...

A film may be your vision, but your vision is likely to get a little clouded by the process. Thus, it is important to get outside opinions on your film. It is equally important to know when to listen to those opinions and when to disregard them.

How to Do It Right...

After you spend a long time on a movie, from the script to development, to fundraising, to casting, through pre-production, shooting and then through several edits, it is absolutely impossible to maintain almost any sort of objectivity. The mere fact that you are involved in the movie on any level means you have lost a good deal of your objectivity. It also means all the other people who had any involvement in the film have lost their objectivity. This is not to say that their opinions are invalid. Good feedback is good feedback no matter what the source—objective or not. The point is merely that opinion becomes tainted by first-hand experiences. Thus, you must turn to others to help you gain back some semblance of objectivity.

Regardless of the source, it's great to hear positive feedback, and knowing what to keep is as important as knowing what to cut. However, it is the critical feedback you must really listen to and consider. You must always be willing to listen and at least consider any feedback from any source before determining its validity. And if you are getting any sort of feedback consistently from multiple sources, there is an excellent chance that it should be seriously considered.

It can be difficult to hear feedback that is critical in nature, but remember, it is the critical feedback that will help your movie the most. The more constructive criticism you take while editing your movie, the less negative feedback you are likely to get from audiences after the movie is done. So be grateful for criticism early in the process, preferably while you can still change things.

Many movies have been drastically reworked utilizing feedback from test screenings. The first cut of the Mel Brooks comedy *Young Frankenstein* was nearly twice as long as the final version of the film. Virtually everyone involved thought the film was a tremendous failure. Mel himself said that "for every joke that worked, there were three that fell flat."[6] Only after test screenings did Mel cut all the jokes that weren't getting laughs from the test audiences, and the movie grew into the comic classic it now is.

Keep in mind that an audience has a vibe, and you should do multiple test screenings, whether formal or informal. Renting out a theater or getting a group of friends together in your living room is a very different experience. For my comedy *Made for Each Other*, we did test screenings for friends, colleagues, comedy fans, college students, and one to a theater full of mostly homeless people and senior citizens (that's who showed up for a Tuesday morning screening). It is entirely possible for the same movie to play great one night and bomb the next and an audience can surprise you (the seniors and homeless people loved *Made for Each Other*). Do not feel forced to let one opinion or one screening make up your mind, but do feel forced to at least consider them carefully. You have to attempt to stay objective to feedback—even though you aren't objective to the movie itself.

Key Points

- Your involvement in the many stages of the process clouds your objectivity to judge your film.
- Those involved in the movie in any form lack true objectivity.
- Outside feedback is critical to gaining an objective perspective.
- Critical feedback is the most productive.
- If you get a particular piece of feedback fairly consistently, there's a good chance it is true.
- Test screenings and audience feedback can spawn great ideas on how to drastically improve a film.
- Every screening is different and feedback may vary, so multiple screenings are helpful.
- You have to attempt to objectively decipher feedback that is helpful from feedback that should be disregarded.
- You must always be willing to consider feedback of any nature.

More Post-Production

Fuck-Up #57

"Post Sound Isn't as Important as Picture"

Why this is a completely naïve thought

"The mind is for seeing, the heart is for hearing."
—Saudi Arabian Proverb

The Fuck-Up...

Sound places us in another world—a world that works in close conjunction with the picture but is capable of taking our ears well beyond where our eyes can go.

As discussed in *Fuck-Up #41: "Sound Is Not Important,"* it is a mistake to think of movies as primarily a "visual medium." Sound is at least 50 percent of the film-going experience. And at least 50 percent of that audio experience will be created in post-production.

How to Do It Right...

Find a horror movie or even a horror movie trailer that you find scary. Watch it. Then watch it again on mute. Afterwards, ask yourself what it was that actually frightened you. Chances are, it was what you heard rather than what you saw. You heard the creaking of an old house; the moody rain of a brooding storm; an abrupt noise that made you jump; or a myriad of other unworldly screams, screeches, and terrifying noises. All those things are part of the magic of sound design.

Horror movies are only one genre that owes an incredible debt to sound design; the same can be said for every genre. (More sarcastic readers might ask, "What about silent films?" Even those films still owe a debt to the mood created by the sparseness of their sound.) A look at recent winners for the Academy Award for Best Sound, an award given to sound designers, includes action films (*The Bourne Ultimatum, The Hurt Locker*), musicals (*Dreamgirls*), dramas (*Ray, Slumdog Millionaire*), action epics (*King Kong, Lord of the Rings: The Return of the King*), war movies (*Saving Private Ryan*), and so on. All these movies are as great as they are in large part due to their remarkable sound design.

Sound affects us both on conscious and subconscious levels. You may be well aware of the loud boom that makes you jump out of your seat, but are you aware of the subtle ambience an empty room makes? If you are truly engaged in a movie, much of its sound will have an effect on you that you are never meant to notice, and that's where its power lies.

The sound designer lives in and creates a world that is both subconscious and conscious. As always, as a filmmaker, you must manipulate the audience without reminding them they are being manipulated. Reaching the subconscious is the real goal of immersive filmmaking. Thus, it is a huge mistake to take your movie's sound design lightly. The audio world of your film must be treated with as much importance as the visual world you create, if not more so. Which leads us to our next *Fuck-Up*...

Key Points

- Film is both a visual and audible medium.
- Much of the emotion of any scene likely comes from the sound.
- A lot of your movie's sound will be created in post-production.
- Every genre of filmmaking owes a tremendous debt to sound.
- Sound affects the listener on conscious and subconscious levels.

Fuck-Up #58

"Anyone with a Computer Can Do Post-Sound"

What work needs to be done and who should do it

"If you think it's expensive to hire a professional to do the job, wait until you hire an amateur."[1]
—Red Adair, oil well firefighter

The Fuck-Up...

On my first movie, I convinced a music editor that he should do all of my post-sound. He was reluctant, but he had the software and was willing to work cheap, so in my mind he was the right guy for the job. This was a classic first-timer mistake that nearly ruined my movie.

How to Do It Right...

Poor sound quality makes an audience uncomfortable. It really does not matter how great everything else about your movie is; an audience will simply not be able to enjoy your film if the sound is unpleasant. If the sound is muffled, low, unclear, full of static, difficult to understand, or otherwise unpleasant in any way, the audience will have a hard time enjoying your film. Thus, it is incredibly important that you have experienced, capable, and talented individuals handling your post-production sound needs.

As with many aspects of filmmaking, the digital age has made post-sound accessible to an increasingly wide range of people at nearly all budget levels. It is even possible to do nearly all your post-sound editing and effects in someone's home Pro Tools setup. This can be a truly great and cost-effective approach; however, what you cannot compromise is the talent of the person doing the work. Just because someone has a Pro Tools setup does not mean she is a capable sound designer or sound editor.

> **THE LINGO**
>
> **Pro Tools:** Popular software used to record, build, and edit soundtracks.
>
> **Soundtrack:** Many people think "soundtrack" only refers to music. However the soundtrack actually refers to all the *sound* mixed together in a film including music, dialogue, and effects.

Make sure the individuals you have handling your post-sound are experienced. Listen to samples of their prior film work. Does their work sound professional or amateur? Are they able to create the type of sound design you want? Do they get the feel of the film that you're going for? Having talented people handling your post-sound can make an amateur film feel far more professional. And having untalented people can make a professional film feel amateur.

There are several steps to post-production sound, and whether a dozen different people handle them or one person handles them all, they must be left in capable hands—and ears.

Let's examine what these jobs are:

- **Sound Designers:** They build the audio landscape of a film and oversee all post-sound work. They design the audible world much in the same way the director, D.P., and production designer build your visual world.
- **Dialogue Editors:** As the name suggests, they edit the dialogue sound. It's their job to make sure all the dialogue sounds natural and is timed well. It can be jarring to have dialogue that sounds as though it was recorded in different locations or with different microphones, so they'll need to smooth it all out. They time the sound to fit the picture and to match the actors' lip movements when nonoriginal dialogue is used. They also preset levels to make sure everyone can be heard, whether it is a whisper or a yell.

- **Effect Editors:** They focus on effects in the same way the dialogue editors focus on dialogue. They build all the sound effects for a film—from the faint sound of wind in the background to large explosions and absolutely every other sound effect you hear.
- **Music Editors:** They edit the composer's score, nonoriginal music, and any other music soundtrack elements, often making pieces shorter, longer, or tailored to key moments in the scene.
- **Mixers:** After all the elements have been compiled and edited, mixers set the final levels or what's called "the final mix." They have final rule over what stays, what goes, what gets heard, where in the room it gets heard (which can vary in a surround sound versus stereo mix), and how well it gets heard.

> **THE LINGO**
>
> **Original music:** New songs created for the movie.
>
> **Nonoriginal music:** Songs used in a movie that were not originally created for the film.

> **THE LINGO**
>
> **Surround sound:** A process that enables the audience to experience sound coming at them from all directions.
>
> **Stereo:** A process that enables the audience to experience sound from two directions (left and right).

Although it is completely possible to do a great deal of post-sound editing and design in fairly inexpensive prosumer setups, I strongly advise against doing your final mix in this manner. The only way to know what your final product will sound like in an actual theater is to mix it in a proper mixing room. This can be an expensive investment, but cutting this corner is another rookie mistake. You've worked too hard on your movie to get to the last step in the puzzle and have a mix that doesn't sound as good as your movie deserves, so let this be one corner you do not cut.

Key Points

- Equipment alone does not make someone qualified to do post-sound.
- Post-sound is incredibly important to how your movie will be perceived.
- Most, but not all, of post-sound work can be done inexpensively by capable professionals on home systems.
- A film's final mix should be done in a professional mixing room.
- You must have capable, experienced people do your post-sound work.

Fuck-Up #59

"Dialogue Is Recorded on Set"

What looping is and why it will save your movie

"If at first you don't succeed, destroy all evidence that you tried."
—author unknown

The Fuck-Up...

Discovering looping is like finding a fairy godmother who has come to grant many of your wishes about what you would like changed in your movie. However, the fuck-up many new filmmakers make is not appreciating what looping is and its capabilities.

Through looping, you can replace poorly recorded or poorly acted sound, and you can change the tone of dialogue or put in new dialogue entirely. By understanding looping, you may be able to radically alter a great deal in your movie (without costly reshoots).

How to Do It Right...

Looping, also called Automated Dialogue Replacement (ADR), is a system in post-production by which an actor replaces dialogue from production or records new dialogue entirely. During a looping session, an actor watches part of the movie on-screen and speaks into a microphone, trying to line up the lip motions of the new audio to the existing picture. An engineer, aided by computer technology, can help subtly manipulate the sound to further match it to the pre-existing lip motions. Looping has become so popular that many of the movies made in Hong Kong have stopped recording any location sound at all and rely solely on looping to put in all the movie's dialogue.

Frequently, while watching a movie or TV show, you will see a wide shot of a car driving down the street. You don't see the actors, but you hear them talking, giving a plot point such as "This is the hideout," "I think Joey is the killer," or some other little bit of exposition. If you are hearing dialogue over a long shot, an establishing shot of a location, on a

> **THE LINGO**
>
> **Establishing shot:** A shot that establishes the location in which a scene will be taking place.
>
> Example: On sitcoms, you often see an establishing shot of a real building before cutting to a set built on a soundstage. This tells the audience that the set is supposed to be located inside the established building.

character's back, or off-camera in another fashion, there is an excellent chance the filmmakers are trying to fix a story problem by adding new dialogue that was not recorded during shooting.

The Coen brothers praised Sam Elliot's mustache in *The Big Lebowski* because the manner in which it obscured his mouth made it particularly easy to change his dialogue in looping. And hey, if you can rewrite your narrator's lines, well, possibilities are limitless. However, looping isn't just for adding in dialogue when you cannot see the actors' mouths. Looping technology has evolved to make it possible to put new words into characters' mouths with near-perfect lip sync—and that is a powerful thing.

If you get creative, looping can provide a much cheaper alternative for fixing problems than reshoots. Have a confusing plot point? You can sneak in a line that clears it up. Want to change a line or even just the line's delivery? You can make something serious that was sarcastic, sarcastic that was serious, happy that was sad, or even give a character an entire new accent he didn't have while shooting.

Looping is a great tool, but there are cautionary reasons why you should not over rely on it. Many talented actors find looping difficult. In those cases, having lengthy looping sessions in which actors struggle to match the timing of their own mouth is an excruciating process. We have all seen examples of movies where the dialogue does not quite seem to match the lips of the actors speaking. This lack of synchronization immediately makes your movie laughable (and not necessarily in a good way).

Furthermore, recapturing the emotion that was present on set may prove difficult, resulting in a poorer performance during looping. The other actors, sets, and wardrobe all aid an actor in creating a performance. This can be difficult to re-create when locked in a box with only a microphone for company. This is why, as with most of filmmaking, you are better off if you can get what you really want while shooting.

One example of intensive looping is Tom Hanks's performance in *Cast Away*. The film shot mostly on real beaches where the near-constant sound of crashing waves made the production sound largely unusable. Approximately an hour and a half of that movie's sound had to be replaced in post-production. This means that nearly half of Tom Hanks's entire Oscar-nominated performance was looped. If you can get quality sound during production, do so. And if you realize during your own shooting that you will absolutely have to loop a scene later, embrace your limitations and get your scene shot—knowing that looping is there to save you.

Key Points

- Looping (also called ADR) is a process in post-production in which you replace old dialogue or create new dialogue entirely.
- Looping can be used to replace poor-quality sound, to change a line's performance, or to add new dialogue.
- Looping can save your movie—if used well.
- Looping is a cost-effective alternative to reshoots when you're looking for a way to change elements of your film.
- Looping can become a dangerous crutch if overly relied upon.
- Whenever possible, get the job done right during shooting and use looping only when necessary.

Fuck-Up #60

"We Can Use Famous Songs"

The danger of getting your heart set on popular music

"Music is everybody's possession. It's only publishers who think that people own it."[2]
—John Lennon

The Fuck-Up…

Music sounds better with familiarity. Without a doubt, songs are more enjoyable when you've heard them before, and the songs we enjoy most are the ones we are familiar with. Thus, it's easy to fall in love with the idea of having familiar songs in our films. However, the cost and difficulty of obtaining the legal rights to use popular songs far too often crushes filmmakers' dreams of using the songs they love.

How to Do It Right…

There is a good chance that you will use some popular music to create the "temp track" to your movie. Finding good temp music greatly helps you get a sense of how scenes will work after music is put in. In fact, the temp music may work so well that you may decide you'd like to keep it permanently. However, purchasing music copyrights is notoriously expensive and difficult. In fact, many independent films have infamously spent as much money clearing music as they spent shooting the entire film.

If you are making a movie on a modest budget, I strongly encourage you to once again face the reality that you will likely need to part with something you love: popular songs in your movie. However, if you are absolutely set on using a popular recording of a popular song, be prepared for the undertaking that comes along with that. There are at least two sets of licenses that you (or your producer, music supervisor, or lawyer) will need to obtain:

> **THE LINGO**
>
> **Temp track:** Temporary music used during editing, which is intended to be replaced later.

> **THE LINGO**
>
> **Music supervisor:** Person hired to handle the finding, negotiating, and licensing of music for a film.

- **Synchronization license:** Obtained from the music publisher, it allows you to use the musical composition (a.k.a. the written music). One of the three major music publishers is likely to control the rights to the songs you want: ASCAP, BMI, or Sesac. To find out which one controls the synchronization licensing rights to any song, visit their websites: www.ascap.com, www.bmi.com, and www.sesac.com.
- **Master use license:** This license allows you to use a particular recording of a song. It's generally obtained through the recording company that released the version of the song you want.

To put this in simpler terms, the sync license has to do with who wrote the song and the master use license has to do with who recorded it (which may or may not have been the same people).

In some cases, you may also need to obtain a performance license (usually not necessary in the United States) or a videogram license for DVD and video usage of a song. These can also be obtained via the music publisher. You should aim to get them as well to make sure you are covered just in case. Furthermore, you should consult with a lawyer as you obtain music licenses because this is one of the more notoriously legally tricky parts of filmmaking.

One option to save some money is to re-record the song you want. You will still have to buy the copyright to the written music (the synchronization license), but you will not need to purchase the copyright to a specific recording of it (the master use license) because you're going to make your own recording. This can save a lot of money, but you risk losing the charm of the original recording. Ever been in a restaurant or store and heard a popular song that didn't sound quite right? The reason is likely that companies, in an effort to save money, have re-recorded the song in order to buy only one set of rights.

You also can save some money by limiting where and how you'll show the movie. When clearing music rights, you can specify where you intend to show the film, on what media, and for what duration of time. All these factors will affect the asking price for the rights. Are you buying the rights for theatrical, TV, and DVD? For North America or the entire globe? For a year or forever? Will your movie's only theatrical showings be in film festivals? Wide theatrical rights cost more than just DVD/Home Video rights. North American rights are cheaper than "buying the world" (meaning everywhere). Rights for a short time period are cheaper than rights that last forever. If you do not know where your movie will be shown or for how long, you can buy some rights now and some later. You can even buy some rights now with an "option" that sets up a predetermined price for other rights should you need them in the future.

Often filmmakers will purchase only "festival rights" for their music. Festival rights come at a very discounted rate and allow you to have the song in your movie for a specified number of film festivals only. The idea here is that because the song is so great, you think it can help you sell your movie. And you hope that when a distributor comes in and buys your film, it will be willing to purchase the rest of the song's licenses that you could not previously afford. Record companies and music publishers will generally sell festival rights fairly cheap with the hope that they will get better money down the road should the movie sell to a distributor. They may be right, but they may be wrong—and the same goes for your own dream about a distributor's willingness to pay for your music.

A distributor might be willing to pay for the song, but more likely it will be unwilling to shell out the cash and decide to leave you with the bill. In the end, you may still end up replacing the song when the distributor refuses to cover such costs. And this situation will be even pricier than if you had replaced the song to begin with, because you will now have to redo your movie's sound mix.

Worse yet, distributors may be turned off to hear that your movie is not ready for distribution because it contains unlicensed music. For this reason, they may not purchase the film at all or claim that you have failed to deliver because the film's producers are ultimately responsible for such clearances.

The reality is that it is rare for a distributor to be willing to pay for music licenses. The safest bet is to cope with the loss of a popular song early. In the end, you're likely to discover there are less popular songs out there that can still work wonderfully for your film—possibly even better once given the chance.

Key Points

- Getting your heart set on a popular song in your movie is likely to lead to heartbreak.
- Clearing music rights is a notoriously expensive and slow process.
- To use a popular recording of a song, you must obtain at least two licenses (synchronization and master use).
- You can re-record a popular song to avoid purchasing the master use license.
- Limiting where and how your film will be seen may help you get a lower price on music licenses.
- You can choose to purchase only festival rights for your music.
- It is unlikely that a distributor will want to pay to clear your music.
- Having unlicensed music in your film may prevent its sale and/or distribution.
- If you aren't sure whether you'll be able to license a song, the best approach is to replace that song with something you can license—and to do so as early as possible.

Fuck-Up #61

"We Can't Afford Good Music"

How to get music cheap, but not cheap sounding

"Music is the shorthand of emotion."[3]
—Leo Tolstoy

The Fuck-Up…

Audiences will not accept flashing signs on the screen telling them to "cry here," "laugh now," or "get excited." However, they will absolutely accept your music's ability to give these very cues.

We all know movies are fiction and we're being lied to; we simply want to be lied to convincingly—without too much attention being drawn to the act of the lying. Score is one of your best tools for stirring emotion without the audience becoming consciously aware they are being manipulated. Good music makes people feel what you want them to feel, and bad music thoroughly ruins that emotion. Thus, regardless of your budget, you need good music.

Unfortunately, filmmakers for many low-budget movies think they cannot afford good music, so they hire a composer who does an amateur-sounding job. This, in turn, makes the whole movie feel amateur.

How to Do It Right…

Around the turn of the millennium, a trend started online of recutting movie trailers with different music to make them into new genres: cutting a comedy with horror music, a drama with an action score, and countless examples of all types of movies cut to the *Brokeback Mountain* score. None of the images or dialogue changed, just the score, and suddenly the films took on completely new meanings. This is a great illustration of the musical score's role in telling the audience what type of movie they are watching and how changing the score completely changes the feel, emotion, and meaning of that experience.

> **THE LINGO**
> **Score:** A movie's original music.

Unless you're making a music video, it's the music's job to serve the movie—not the other way around. You must score closely to picture, finding emotional beats and underlining them musically without overemphasizing them to the point where the manipulation draws attention to itself. Soon you may find that a scene that was painful to watch without a score works wonderfully with it.

Be aware, however, that too much music can backfire. This is another pitfall first-time filmmakers frequently fall into. We all love music, but it is absolutely possible to have too much of a good thing. Not having music for a while in a film makes it more satisfying when it eventually comes in. Perhaps the most famous example of this phenomenon is John Williams's score for *Jaws*. Two simple notes became the theme that represented the infamous shark. At first, those two notes let the audience know when the shark is near. Later in the movie, the notes tease us with the shark's presence, and then the tension is relieved as we realize the music misled us and the shark is, in fact, not around. Still later in the movie, we are shocked when the shark suddenly appears without the warning of the music alerting us in the manner we'd been set up to expect. As John Williams effectively proved, both utilizing and denying score can be very effective.

Although good music is important, it need not necessarily be expensive. Many great musical scores have been made inexpensively. Talented composers, armed with the right technology, can make an entire score digitally without bringing in and recording live musicians. Some digital music libraries do a surprisingly good job of fabricating what live musicians sound like. And many great scores have been done with only a few instruments. The real key to scoring is to figure out what works best for your film and budget. Would a simple score of only a few digital instruments work? Do you need a live 400-piece symphony orchestra? Find a composer and approach that fits your movie, style, and budget. Most important of all, never compromise quality for quantity (or any other factor). A small professional-sounding score will serve your movie vastly better than a large score of amateur quality.

I assure you there are many talented and capable composers out there who would be excited to score your movie—and will do a professional-sounding job. Do not settle for anything less than your movie deserves. Interview as many composers as you can to figure out whose style, sensibilities, and budget demands work best for your film. You may be surprised to find out just how much the right composer can inexpensively accomplish for your film. A good score will immensely affect whether or not your movie feels cheap; so when it comes to your movie's soundtrack, always maintain a high level of quality control.

Key Points

- An audience wants to be emotionally manipulated, but they don't want attention drawn to that manipulation.
- Music is a great tool for manipulating the audience's emotion.
- The music must serve the movie, never the other way around.
- Your score should closely follow and underline the emotional beats of your film.
- Too much music can backfire.
- Good music need not be expensive.
- There are many options for how to score your film. Find the best approach for your film and your budget.
- There are many options of who can score your film. Don't settle for anything other than the best fit for the job.

Fuck-Up #62

"Cinematography Happens While Shooting"

The magic of color correction

"The chief aim of colour should be to serve expression as well as possible."[4]

—Matisse

The Fuck-Up...

Most moviegoers are completely unaware color correction exists. Furthermore, most people working in film don't truly understand just how much a movie's look can drastically change during this incredible process. By not appreciating the power of color correction, you risk missing out on your last chance to reshape the look and feel of your movie.

How to Do It Right...

With color correction, you can alter the visual look and feel of your movie, long after you shoot it. This may involve subtle changes such as matching the lighting from one shot to another or improving an actor's skin tone. It also may be more noticeable changes, such as making a scene's color palette warmer, cooler, darker, or brighter to affect the visual emotion therein. Or the color correction may be responsible for drastically altering the entire visual style of your movie, such as by making scenes that were shot in bright sunlight feel dark and high contrast.

Many directors and D.P.s rely on the color correction stage to completely set the look and stylization of their movies. This can mean taking the visuals of your movie into completely new territories from the way it was originally shot. Highly stylized films like *300* and *Sin City* find their dramatic looks in the color correction stage.

For most films, you probably do not want to create a new look but rather want to tweak and improve the film's existing look. Color correction allows you to improve image quality, change lighting, make a character look better, or make a character look worse—all within the pre-existing visuals of your particular movie. I have used color correction to make dead grass appear green, tone down the appearance of makeup, give actors healthier skin tones, wipe away years of aging, and even remove gray hairs.

To examine color correction further, let's look at some examples. We'll start with Figure 62.1 as our un-color-corrected starting point and play with a few corrections to see how we can change its look and feel. **Please note: For full color of the following four images, please see the insert after this chapter.**

One approach, popular in edgy horror films and gritty thrillers, is to give the movie a "bleach bypass" look. This entails increasing the contrast, lowering the saturation, and crushing the blacks. You can see an example of this sort of color correction in Figure 62.2.

THE LINGO

Bleach bypass: A system to give a film a high-contrast and low-saturation look. It was obtained originally by skipping the bleaching process during film development. For movies not shot on film, it is often simulated during color correction.

For a romance, you might want to create a happy, "warm" feeling, so you could increase the saturation and create brighter, warmer colors. For an example of that sort of correction, check out the color treatment in Figure 62.3.

Alternatively, to give the same image a look more appropriate for a dream sequence, you could consider boosting the saturation, using what is called "selective luminance grading," and letting the highlights bloom, as is the case with the correction done for Figure 62.4.

As you can see by these few examples, color correction can give the same image many different looks and feels. These examples represent just a few of the infinite possibilities color correction gives you to

For full color of the following four images, please see the insert after this chapter.

Figure 62.1 *Original image before color correction. For full color image please see page 2 of the insert. (Photo by Rachel Utain-Evans.)*

Figure 62.2 *Color corrected for a "bleach bypass" look. For full color image please see page 2 of the insert. (Color correction by Will Hong. Photo by Rachel Utain-Evans.)*

Figure 62.3 *Color corrected for a warm, romantic look. For full color image please see page 3 of the insert. (Color correction by Will Hong. Photo by Rachel Utain-Evans.)*

Figure 62.4 *Color corrected for a saturated dream-like look. For full color image please see page 3 of the insert. (Color correction by Will Hong. Photo by Rachel Utain-Evans.)*

change the look and feel of your movie. Furthermore, if you find these differences drastic on still images, I assure you they are vastly more impressive when applied to moving images.

The greatest influence over the quality of your color correction is not the software, but the skill level of the artist doing the correction and the amount of time they have to do their work. An expensive system manned by someone unskilled is much less valuable than a talented artist with a less expensive correction system really putting the time and effort into her work. Whether you are doing your color correction on your home computer or on a high-end system, the work will only ever be as good as the artist doing the correction, the time she has to do the work, and the footage available to work with.

Although color correction is indeed powerful, as with all post-production tools, the advice remains the same: if you can accomplish what you want while shooting rather than trying to fix it in post-production, do so. Always aim to obtain as close to the final desired look as possible while shooting. Doing so is the best way to guarantee you'll love the final look of your movie.

Key Points

- Color correction is one of the most underappreciated facets of the filmmaking process.
- Color correction allows filmmakers to subtly tweak and improve the existing look of their film.
- Through color correction, you can match shots; alter lighting and colors; fix actors' skin tones; add or remove contrast, saturation, and brightness; and much more.
- Color correction can also be used to radically change the look of a film.
- Color correction is only as good as the colorist doing the work.
- Always aim to achieve your desired look as much as possible while shooting.

Fuck-Up #63

"I Gotta Have Effects!"

When to use visual effects and what to expect

"Things should be made as simple as possible, but not any simpler."[5]
—Albert Einstein

The Fuck-Up...

New filmmakers often become so enamored with visual effects that they forget the effects are supposed to serve the movie—not the other way around. This is a remarkably common first-timer mistake, which frequently hurts the film and comes to be regretted.

How to Do It Right...

Filmmaker Kerry Conran shot his short film *The World of Tomorrow* entirely in his apartment in front of a green screen. He then spent the next four years creating the visual effects to complete the six-minute film. The success of that short landed him the feature-length version of the film, titled *Sky Captain and the World of Tomorrow* starring Jude Law, Gwyneth Paltrow, and Angelina Jolie. Films like Mr. Conran's proved that visual effects can be an unbelievable resource for filmmakers at all budget levels. Of course, for Conran, this was possible because he had the skills to accomplish it—and more importantly, he developed a project designed to exploit the resources and skills he already had.

Conran was technically savvy enough to accomplish his own effects, and if you and your team have such resources, you should certainly embrace and exploit them. However, if you do not have the resources to pull off visual effects convincingly, the results are likely to be better if you create something in front of the camera or lose those shots entirely. While there are no doubt amazing feats of computer generated imagery (CGI), the odds of a practical (meaning real, not computer-generated) effect looking more, well, "real" is high. And this theory is exponentially more true in the world of lower budget filmmaking. Poor-quality visual effects have become a trademark of bad movies in recent years—for an example, watch almost any SyFy channel original movie.

This is not to say you should be anti-CGI. CGI has opened up a whole new world of filmmaking that never would have been possible in pre-CGI days: lifelike dinosaurs walking among us, epic war battles with thousands of combatants, and many other unique visual experiences far removed from our own reality. However, this power can be dangerous if overused. You have to wonder: if they could have animated the original Yoda instead of a using a Muppet, would it have had the same charm? If the shark in *Jaws* could have been animated, as would likely be the case today, would we have seen too much of it? Or worse yet, would it have looked real enough to scare us?

As we have seen time and time again, our limitations are frequently what spawn the best creativity. In a computer-generated world, we are literally limited only by our imagination. However, the size of our imaginations may not always align with the quality of our CGI. *Jurassic Park* is often credited with changing the way movies utilize CGI, so allow me to quote Jeff Goldblum's character

Sheet #: 2 1pg	Scene: 2	EXT	Bar Guy walks out of bar.	Day	1
Sheet #: 3 1pg	Scene: 3	EXT	Street Guy walks down street and meets Other Guy.	Night	1, 3
End of Day 1 - Friday, February 17, 2015.			**Pg total: 2**		
Sheet #: 1 1pg	Scene: 1	INT	Bar Guy walks in to bar.	Day	1, 2
Sheet #: 4 1pg	Scene: 4	INT	Room Guy and Other Guy go into room	Night	1, 3
End of Day 2 - Saturday, February 18, 2015.			**Pg total: 2**		

Figure 23.1 *Sample stripboard.*

Figure 62.1 *Original image before color correction. (Photo by Rachel Utain-Evans.)*

Figure 62.2 *Color corrected for a "bleach bypass" look. (Color correction by Will Hong. Photo by Rachel Utain-Evans.)*

Figure 62.3 *Color corrected for a warm, romantic look. (Color correction by Will Hong. Photo by Rachel Utain-Evans.)*

Figure 62.4 *Color corrected for a saturated dream-like look. (Color correction by Will Hong. Photo by Rachel Utain-Evans.)*

Dr. Malcolm from that movie, who accused the scientists of being "so preoccupied with whether or not they could, they didn't stop to think if they should." The same goes for considering CGI in your film; anything *can* be done—*should* it be done is a question to be considered more carefully.

Regardless of whether you believe visual effects to be creatively liberating or restraining, no CGI is almost always better than bad CGI. Remember, films are fiction, but your audience wants to be lied to *well*. If they cannot allow themselves to believe what you are fabricating, it can hurt their movie-going experience. So wield your power carefully.

The safest approach is to know the limitations and capabilities of the VFX you intend to utilize. Do tests if you can. Listen to the people who will help create your VFX; they will no doubt be able to tell you what will make the effects look better. If they suggest making something a night scene or adding more shadows, and your script will allow for it, do it. If you are able to successfully use VFX in your movie, realize it is a truly amazing and powerful tool and one that you should fully exploit. And if you do not have the resources to effectively achieve certain effects, that, too, is worth considering.

Key Points

- Visual effects have opened up infinite possibilities of visuals that filmmakers can create.
- When considering visual effects, you should carefully examine both your ability to accomplish them convincingly and how they will serve your movie.
- You are likely to get better results creating effects in front of the camera rather than in post, if possible. This theory tends to be even more relevant at lower budget levels.
- No CGI is likely to be preferable to bad CGI.
- By exploring your limitations, you will figure out what is possible and discover the visual effects to improve your film.
- Effects should not come at the expense of the movie as a whole.

Life after Post-Production

Fuck-Up #64

"The Movie's Done; I'm Done"

Why finishing the film is part of your journey, not the destination

"My play was a complete success. The audience was a failure."[1]
—Ashleigh Brilliant

The Fuck-Up...

Making a movie is a lengthy, arduous, and exhausting process. By the time you actually finish your film, there's a good chance you'll be fairly sick of it and relieved the process is almost over. The problem is, you're not at the end of your journey.

Finishing your movie is quite the accomplishment, but it does not mean your work is done. Far too many filmmakers insist they just want to focus on completing their movie and then never actually do anything with the completed film. Surely, you did not go through all the hard work it took to get a movie made to have only you and your friends watch it. Furthermore, your investors would probably like you to at least try to make some of their money back—which is also your best hope of getting to make your next movie.

How to Do It Right...

Over the next few *Fuck-Ups*, we'll discuss strategies for getting your movie sold, distributed, and marketed. As you embark on this new stage in your film's life, be prepared that the road ahead may still be lengthy. One of the more common (and annoying) questions filmmakers are often asked is, "What's taking so long?" Those who have never experienced an independent film's journey from script to screen and beyond seem to be under the impression that shortly after you finish shooting they should able to go to their local theater and see the movie. Which would be wonderful—if only it were true.

While studio movies are made with release dates in place, independent films are likely to embark on a search for distribution only after they are completed, and that takes time. Shopping a movie to festivals and distributors can take months or even years. After that, many movies infamously sit on a distributor's shelf awaiting distribution for many more months, years, or (as is any film-maker's worst nightmare) forever. After a release date is set, marketing and distribution can like-wise be a time-consuming process. And after that, it will be even longer until the residual checks (if there are any) finally start coming in. In other words, it's going to be awhile. So be patient and don't lose enthusiasm; you're still going to need it. You've worked hard to get your movie to where it is. All that hard work deserves the best chance possible at paying off. You need to keep on fighting, taking key steps to get your film sold, distributed, and to as wide an audience as possible. Celebrate finishing your film, but know there's more hard work to come.

Key Points

- Finishing a movie does not mean your work is done.
- Making sure a film finds an audience is its own challenging stage.
- Selling, marketing, and distributing a film can be a lengthy process. Prepare yourself for the long haul.

Fuck-Up #65

"I'll Submit to Festivals and Then Await Success"

Why this isn't enough of a plan

"There's only one list that's more illustrious than the list of directors who won the Palme d'Or. It's the list of directors who didn't."[2]
—Quentin Tarantino

The Fuck-Up...

Many filmmakers make movies with the end goal being "we'll submit to film festivals." How-ever, submitting your film to top festivals and then simply awaiting fame and recognition is as likely to work out as any other Hollywood fairytale. For every festival success, there is a lot more happening behind the scenes than just the happy ending we all read and dream about. Submitting to festivals and merely awaiting success is not nearly enough of a plan.

How to Do It Right...

It seems that virtually every city, neighborhood, community center, and chicken shack in America now has a "film festival." Some are prestigious, and others more closely resemble some guy screening movies in the basement of his mom's house. This makes talking about film festivals a bit tricky because there is an incredible difference between screening your movie at Cannes versus the Lower Southern Punxsutawney Film Festival and Pig Roast.

The reason film festivals continue to pop up everywhere is that they've become incredibly trendy, which can be a very good thing for you and your movie. Attending some festivals and perhaps garnering a few awards can help give your movie prestige. However, it could also prove to be a waste of time because it is unlikely that distributors looking to buy films attend the abundance of smaller festivals out there. As is nearly always the case, the key is to know what you want. If your goal is to have people see your movie or to put some laurel logos on your poster, there is no bad audience. However, if your goal is the sale of your film to distributors, some festivals are undoubtedly better than others.

The irony behind some of the more famous film festivals is that what at one time made them so trendy—being a showcase for independent films—has, to a large degree, gone the opposite direction. Many festivals have come to represent, in many ways, what they started off in opposition to: the Hollywood system. Nearly all the major festivals now devote a significant part of their programming to be utilized as marketing tools for studio films. A good percent of movies at any of the top festivals are not looking for distribution, but rather using the festival as part of their multinational high-profile marketing campaigns. Even the term "independent film" has strayed far away from its original meaning. "Independent" used to refer to a movie being financed independently from the major studios. Now it refers more to a genre than a financing model.

To further the irony, many of the major studios have "independent" branches for producing and purchasing movies (although many of these branches began closing in the early 2000s). Companies such as Warner Independent, Fox Searchlight, and Sony Pictures Classics are studio owned and financed. Although many of these companies do purchase and distribute films that were truly produced financially independently from a studio, they are still part of major studios and the conglomerates they represent. These companies often buy and distribute independent films, making them both your potential clients as well as potential competitors for festival spots.

Many of the film festivals pride themselves in supporting the "independent" genre while many of the movies they show have already been purchased for distribution by major studios—or were entirely financed by studios from the beginning. This can all seem a bit daunting when you know that buyers are unlikely to attend smaller festivals, and larger festivals fill a lot of their slots with movies that already have distributor backing in place.

Despite the difficulties of finding a good festival home for your film, it's still worth trying a top-down approach. If you can get into a more prestigious film festival, do it. Buyers do attend such festivals, independent movies do get in, and films sell at the major festivals every year. But know going in that virtually everyone who makes an indie film is dreaming of Sundance, and most will have that dream crushed. Should you not get in, continue down your list to second- and third-tier festivals, and so on.

Competition is intense, with the major festivals receiving thousands of submissions competing for what are likely only dozens of spots. Furthermore, the most respected film festivals are intensely political to get into. Even nonstudio movies will get preference if they have powerful agents, producers, or celebrities campaigning for them. Festivals thrive on publicity, so movies with famous talent will get treated more favorably, especially if the stars agree to attend the festival. Festivals will also be far more eager to show your movie if it is a "premiere," which means it has not been shown at any other festivals or by any other means of distribution yet. And like most things in life, it often comes down to whom you know—people pulling strings behind the scenes at a festival frequently decide what gets in. If you have any political strings you can pull at any of the major film festivals or can guarantee a premiere or stars' attendance, I certainly recommend using that leverage because, let's face it, your competition is playing the same game.

If you do get rejected from a festival, do not take it personally. Most submissions are screened by a volunteer trying to wade through endless stacks of movies looking for rare gems. Not getting into a big festival does not mean your movie would not have played well there. It may simply mean the volunteer who watched your movie didn't care for it enough to get it to the next step, where some other volunteer or festival programmer would watch it. One person's opinion may control your fate, but it's just that—one person's opinion. The rejection may also simply mean that your movie doesn't fit into whatever "brand" or direction the programmers are trying to take a particular festival. Often festivals want to change direction or try something new. After all, how many movies can Sundance have about "lonely people finding each other?" (The answer is "a lot.") And the rejection may also mean that you simply could not pull the necessary political strings that other films had, regardless of their quality.

THE LINGO

Festival programmer: The person whose job it is to help select and schedule the films at a festival.

If you do get into a festival, guess what? You're still not guaranteed success. Lots of movies get into the top festivals every year and still never find distribution. After getting in, you must hustle to give yourself the best chance possible at festival success. Try to pull political strings if you have them to assure a good time slot and word of mouth. There is a world of difference between who will show up to a Friday night showing versus one at 9 a.m. on a Tuesday. The same goes for promoting your film at the festival: you must get out there and promote it properly to make sure the right people see and are talking about your movie. Fortunately, this is a task you need not do completely alone. Good publicists and "producer's reps" can help in this regard. Which leads us to our next *Fuck-Up*…

Key Points

- Film festivals can be a great tool for marketing and selling your film.
- Submitting to film festivals alone is no assurance of success.
- There are countless film festivals, and you must know what your goals are to find the right ones for your film.
- Many studio films go to festivals solely for promotion and already have distribution in place.
- Getting into film festivals can be a challenging and very political process.
- A rejection is not necessarily a commentary on your film's quality; many other factors are at play.
- Getting your film accepted to film festivals is no assurance of success.
- When your film is in a film festival, you must continue to fight to make sure you get the right people seeing and talking about your film.

Fuck-Up #66

"This Guy Can Sell My Movie"
How to pick the right person to sell your movie

"Sales are contingent upon the attitude of the salesman, not the attitude of the prospect."[3]
—W. Clement Stone

The Fuck-Up...

A lot of new filmmakers are unaware that there are people whose job is to sell movies to distributors. Thus, a common first-timer mistake is not utilizing these professionals. And, an even worse mistake is committing to the wrong one.

How to Do It Right...

Being a "producer's rep" (short for "producer's representative") is a jack-of-many-trades job, but the goal is always the same: selling movies and making money. That can include many tasks, from ensuring that potential buyers see your movie through negotiating the film's final distribution deal and all the steps that may occur in between.

Producer's representatives used to be called "sales agents," but because both the words "sales" and "agent" carry a somewhat negative connotation, "producer's rep" is now the commonly preferred title. Nevertheless, often those negative connotations are deserved. Many successful (and unsuccessful) producer's reps are known for a cutthroat business mentality. However, this is not necessarily a bad thing. You may find such an approach a necessary tool for a difficult job. Or you may wish to find a producer's rep with a less unsavory approach. Just as when it comes to getting the movie made, when you're selling the movie, the rule is quite often, "any way possible—that you feel comfortable with."

Many producer's reps are entertainment lawyers who sell movies as just one of their specialties. Because so much of selling a film comes down to negotiating the deal, it is easy to see why lawyers are often a good fit for the job. However, it's worth noting that an equal number of successful producer's reps are not lawyers, and you should not use a law degree as a litmus test to decide who's a good rep for your film.

A good rep has relationships with various distributors who might be interested in buying your film. When considering a rep, ask what distributors he has relationships with and, more importantly, to whom he has sold films before. A good rep will also be able to develop a plan to help guide your movie along a path to get distributors aware of, excited about, and interested in possibly releasing your film. Your rep may advise you to enter your film into festivals; to go straight to distributors with screeners or screenings; and/or to put together promotional materials such as posters, trailers, and websites that can be used to show distributors just how marketable your movie truly is. So, ask what type of plan the rep would advise for your film and why.

> **THE LINGO**
>
> **Screeners:** Copies of the movie you send out so that people (such as prospective buyers) can watch at their leisure.
>
> **Screenings:** Inviting people (such as prospective buyers) to come watch a movie at a specified time and place.

There are a handful of true powerhouse producer's reps (we'll call them "big reps"), and there are countless other people who dabble in film sales, hustling and attempting to sell movies with varying degrees of success and validity (we'll call these "small reps"). The debate of whether to go with a big rep, small rep, or something in between is similar to the debate when deciding whether to go with a big agent or small agent to represent you personally. A big rep has more contacts and clout to make a deal happen, and it may be easier for this person to get the "right people" to see your movie. However, this rep may also have bigger projects that are likely to net her a lot more money, and thus the rep will be less motivated to spend significant time and effort working on selling your movie. Some bigger reps are infamous for doing what is referred to in the industry as "hip pocketing." This means they are not really going to devote much energy to your film whatsoever; however, should the filmmakers' own hard work bring in an offer, they'll show up to maybe negotiate the deal and take their cut. Conversely, a smaller rep is less likely to have the same contacts or clout, but there is a better chance she will view you as an important client and spend more time and effort trying to sell your movie. This sort of enthusiasm is great and may or may not prove to be what gets the job done.

Unfortunately, there is absolutely no way to know for certain who is the best rep for your movie. So take as many meetings as you can get and feel out the situation. Hopefully, you will be able to get a sense of whether a prospective rep is sincerely behind the project or just giving the usual "smoke up the ass" routine. If a rep is too busy to take a meeting or returns emails and calls slowly, there's an excellent chance that sort of treatment will continue after she signs on to represent a movie. And if a prospective rep is too green to know what she is doing or is just plain full of it, you will likely get that vibe early on as well. Unfortunately, a lot of people claiming they sell movies aren't all that reliable. As always, trust your gut and go with the best option you can get your hands on.

No matter what rep you go with, you will never be able to completely rely on that individual to sell your film. You must work with him, personally hustling and promoting your movie. As in most stages of filmmaking, if you want something done right, keep a personal hand in making sure things keep moving forward effectively.

There is also something to be said for selling a movie completely on your own. Numerous independent films have been sold without reps attached due solely to the filmmakers' own efforts. Just keep in mind your own abilities: if you feel capable at self-hustling, more power to you (no reason to give away that 10 percent if you don't have to). Try to be aware of what you're signing yourself up for. Can you go about marketing your movie online or at festivals to get distributors interested? Can you get your movie in front of distributors? And can you negotiate your own distribution deal or bring in a lawyer solely for that portion of the process? Figure out what you can pull off yourself and where you should bring in outside help. No matter what, realize that you have to work hard to get a movie made, and you must work equally hard to get that effort rewarded.

Key Points

- The job of a producer's rep is to sell movies to distributors.
- Producer's reps often display varying levels of integrity.
- When picking a rep, you must decide what is right for your particular film.
- A big rep is likely to have better contacts than a smaller rep but spend less effort on any one project.
- A smaller rep is likely to give each project more effort but may not have the same level of industry contacts that a big rep has.
- It is possible to sell a movie yourself.
- Regardless of who your producer's rep is, you must work hard to personally make sure your movie has a chance at the best distribution deal possible.

Fuck-Up #67

"A Distributor Will Pay to Finish the Movie"
The reality of getting a distributor to pay for anything

"If you would know the value of money, go and try to borrow some."[4]
—Benjamin Franklin

The Fuck-Up...

New filmmakers often dream that if they can get their movie to a certain point, some deep-pocketed distributor will open their checkbook to get the movie finished. Although this has occurred in some very rare occasions, the odds of it happening are phenomenally poor. More often distributors simply flee from incomplete movies, and the filmmaker is left with an unfinished film that will never find an audience.

How to Do It Right...

In 2008 IFC Films bought director Steven Soderbergh's dual movies *Che: Part One* and *Che: Part Two* for a deal that was estimated at "low six figures." That price was for two films, which cost approximately $70 million to make, collectively; were directed by an A-list Academy Award–winning director; and starred a high-profile Academy Award–winning actor, Benicio del Toro. The film also won the best actor prize for Del Toro at the Cannes Film Festival and was nominated for the prestigious Golden Palm. Despite the movies' incredible pedigree and critical acclaim, the distributor was unwilling or unable to advance more than the "low six figures" for both films, and this is not the least bit unusual.

> **THE LINGO**
>
> **Advance:** Money paid at the time of sale by a distributor in anticipation of profits.
>
> Example: Every year you hear stories of the rare multimillion-dollar advance for films being bought at Sundance.

The dream that a distributor will want to throw down a lot of advance money for a film is unlikely for an Academy Award–winning director and even less likely for an unknown one. New filmmakers often hope that the distributor will pay to clear all the music for which they could afford only festival rights, pay to fix the soundtrack (a dream popularized when Columbia Pictures put up the money to fix the soundtrack for Robert Rodriguez's *El Mariachi*), or pay to re-edit the film (as was the case for the second theatrical run of Jared Hess's film *Napoleon Dynamite*). Although it is great to dream of the mighty wallet of a distributor stepping in and saving your movie, the truth is, it is very unlikely to happen.

Purchasing a film is already a financial risk for a distributor, and if the film is not in a near-distribution-ready state, it adds additional risk that may deter the distributor from considering taking it on. For your film to have the best chance at a release, you should aim to have it 100 percent complete before taking it to distributors if at all possible.

Having a product that is ready for distribution means both having your movie complete and having all your legal ducks in a row. You're in a much better position if all the music in your film has been cleared; your credit sequences are finalized; and your color correction and sound mix are completed, paid for, and ready to deliver.

Despite ever-shrinking advances from distributors, many independent films still rely on an advance to help them pay for some of the "deliverables" the distributors require. However, the safest bet is to minimize this need. Distributors will require a list of deliverables such as receiving the film and its soundtrack in various formats. There are also

> **THE LINGO**
>
> **Deliverables:** The items required by a distributor to release a film.
>
> Example: "We didn't get paid because the distributor claimed we hadn't fulfilled all our deliverables."

legal deliverables, such as all actor, location, and music clearances as well as chain of title. Distributors are often unwilling to cover deliverable costs entirely. This means that even if your movie is finished, if you cannot afford to create all the items distributors ask for, they may still "reject delivery," in which case they are under no obligation to release your film.

THE LINGO

Chain of title: The history of ownership to a property.

Example: The chain of title started with an idea. That idea was made into a video game. The video game was made into a book. The book was made into a screenplay. And the screenplay was made into a movie.

The safest approach is to not count on a distributor to step in and save your movie. As with many things in life, the surest way to see that something gets done is to do it yourself. You must set out in your budget to finish the movie *completely*, and that means all the way through delivery. And should a distributor step up and provide a healthy advance, even better, you can begin paying back your investors or, just maybe, put any profits toward your next movie.

Key Points

- It is highly unlikely that a distributor will want to give you a large sum of money to finish or improve your movie.
- Having an incomplete film may deter distributors from wanting to take on a movie.
- If you want to make your film appealing to distributors, both the movie itself and your paperwork should be as delivery ready as possible.
- If you can't afford to create deliverables, your movie may never get released.
- You may be able to get an advance from your distributor to help pay for part or all of the costs of creating deliverables, but you should count on it as little as possible.

Fuck-Up #68

"Money, Fame, Power: Here I Come!"

Why it's never easy, no matter how many films you've made

"Renew your passions daily."[5]
—Terri Guillemets

The Fuck-Up...

When new filmmakers set out to make their first movie, they often think that if they can just get this movie made, the acclaim will roll in and be followed by future movie after movie. The reality is that although having a movie under your belt is a huge advantage, you will likely have to keep fighting to get your second, third, or hundredth movie made.

How to Do It Right...

Steven Spielberg set out to make a feature-film adaptation of the beloved comic *Tintin* in 1984. That attempt failed. In 2007, he teamed up with Peter Jackson, the acclaimed director of the *Lord of the Rings* franchise, to once again try to bring *Tintin* to the big screen. Spielberg's old home Dreamworks proved unwilling to take on the project. Universal and Paramount were next to reject Spielberg and Jackson. The film continued to flounder and looked as though it wouldn't get made. Eventually, Sony and Paramount got together, worked out an arrangement to co-finance the $130 million budget, and *Tintin* got a breath of new life. If successful directors of billion-dollar franchises such as Steven Spielberg and Peter Jackson have to struggle and fight to get their movies made, chances are you will, too.

Filmmaking is a dream job, but rarely an easy one. Even well-established directors and producers find themselves constantly fighting for their next film. And very frequently, their films still do not get made. With experience and success, the process may get *easier*, but it rarely actually gets easy. The passion you have as a filmmaker starting out must be the passion you have as a filmmaker at any stage of your career.

Key Points

- Getting movies made is rarely ever easy.
- You need passion to be a filmmaker at any stage.

Fuck-Up #69

"There's No Formula for Success"

A formula for success (really)

"When I let go of what I am, I become what I might be."[6]
—Lao Tzu

The Fuck-Up...

Some people think there's no formula for success. They're wrong. I just so happen to have one, so get your highlighters ready.

How to Do It Right...

Ambition + Talent + Luck = Success

The formula for success is actually that simple, and here's the even better part: if you are lacking in any one of these three factors, you can make up for it by upping the other two. Let's say you are lucky enough to be born into a Hollywood family that is willing to use its connections to help you professionally. Thanks to your high "luck" quotient, you can probably get by being a little less talented *or* ambitious. Or, if you are incredibly talented and very lucky, well then, perhaps you can get by without having to be exceptionally ambitious. And let's say you don't have very much luck; then you had better be talented and ambitious as all hell.

Think about how much you have of each of these three elements and then determine which elements you are going to have to boost to compensate for the ones that fall short. Along the way, avoid the fuck-ups you can, learn from the ones you can't, and let me know how it goes.

Good Luck,

Daryl Bob Goldberg

References

Chapter 1

1. http://www.1-famous-quotes.com/quote/214253 [accessed 12.07.11].
2. http://www.imdb.com/name/nm0000040/bio [accessed 20.07.11].
3. http://www.goodreads.com/quotes/show/311222 [accessed 20.07.11].
4. http://thinkexist.com/quotation/perhaps_it_sounds_ridiculous-but_the_best_thing/220653.html [accessed 20.07.11].
5. http://www.brainyquote.com/quotes/quotes/j/jamescamer360513.html [accessed 20.07.11].
6. http://thinkexist.com/quotation/true_wisdom_comes_to_each_of_us_when_we_realize/259526.html [accessed 20.07.11].
7. http://thinkexist.com/quotation/if_you_want_to_make_god_laugh-tell_him_about_your/226952.html [accessed 20.07.11].
8. http://www.whosdatedwho.com/tpx_2853675/worth/quotes_4 [accessed 20.07.11].
9. http://www.imdb.com/name/nm0000339/bio [accessed 20.07.11].
10. http://thinkexist.com/quotation/adversity_reveals_genius-prosperity_conceals_it/152529.html [accessed 20.07.11].
11. http://www.evancarmichael.com/Famous-Entrepreneurs/629/Steven-Spielberg-Quotes.html [accessed 20.07.11].
12. http://www.poemhunter.com/poem/no-man-is-an-island/ [accessed 20.07.11].
13. http://www.quotationspage.com/quote/2162.html [accessed 20.07.11].

Chapter 2

1. http://thinkexist.com/quotation/to_hell_with_circumstances-i_create_opportunities/151127.html [accessed 20.07.11].
2. http://www.dailycelebrations.com/marketing.htm [accessed 12.07.11].
3. http://thinkexist.com/quotation/faith_is_taking_the_first_step_even_when_you_don/214973.html [accessed 12.07.11].
4. http://www.brainyquote.com/quotes/quotes/o/oscarlevan391476.html [accessed 12.07.11].
5. http://thinkexist.com/quotation/even-a-fool-knows-you-can-t-touch-the-stars-but/348400.html [accessed 13.07.11].
6. http://thinkexist.com/quotation/a_verbal_contract_isn-t_worth_the_paper_it-s/191894.html [accessed 20.07.11].
7. http://quotations.about.com/od/moretypes/a/taxquotes1.htm [accessed 20.07.11].

8. http://www.karlonia.com/2008/07/24/101-funny-quotes-about-money/ [accessed 20.07.11].

9. http://www.indiewire.com/article/2011/07/06/from_the_iw_vaults_sofia_coppola_talks_lost_in_translation_her_love_story_t [accessed 20.07.11].

10. http://www.phrases.org.uk/meanings/tanstaafl.html [accessed 20.07.11].

11. http://www.imdb.com/name/nm0000095/bio [accessed 20.07.11].

12. http://thinkexist.com/quotation/he_who_is_his_own_lawyer_has_a_fool_for_a/180044.html [accessed 20.07.11].

Chapter 3

1. http://thinkexist.com/quotation/he_who_fails_to_plan-plans_to/169985.html [accessed 20.07.11].

2. http://www.culturevulture.net/Television/HitchcockSelznick.htm [accessed 20.07.11].

3. http://www.brainyquote.com/quotes/quotes/t/toddsolond355275.html [accessed 20.07.11].

4. http://www.searchquotes.com/quotation/Casting_is_65_percent_of_directing./68529/ [accessed 20.07.11].

5. http://www.realeyz.tv/en/nina-kusturica-eva-testor-24-realities-per-second_cont4575.html [accessed 20.07.11].

6. http://blog.gaiam.com/quotes/topics/right-tool-right-job [accessed 20.07.11].

7. http://www.brainyquote.com/quotes/quotes/s/suntzu129855.html [accessed 20.07.11].

8. http://thinkexist.com/quotation/tell_me_and_i-ll_forget-show_me_and_i_may/10546.html [accessed 20.07.11].

Chapter 4

1. http://thinkexist.com/quotation/the_key_is_not_to_prioritize_what-s_on_your/220232.html [accessed 20.07.11].

2. http://www.imdb.com/character/ch0001544/quotes [accessed 20.07.11].

Chapter 5

1. http://www.searchquotes.com/quotation/You'd_be_surprised_how_much_it_costs_to_look_this_cheap!/244294/ [accessed 20.07.11].

2. http://www.searchquotes.com/quotation/Everything_is_temporary._Everything_is_bound_to_end./68990/ [accessed 20.07.11].

3. http://memory.loc.gov/ammem/edhtml/edmvhm.html [accessed 20.07.11].

4. http://thinkexist.com/quotation/listen_to_the_mustn-ts-child-listen_to_the_don-ts/151628.html [accessed 20.07.11].

5. http://filmonic.com/tom-cruise-takes-a-pay-cut-for-mission-impossible-4 [accessed 20.07.11].

6. http://thinkexist.com/quotation/it-s_clearly_a_budget-it-s_got_a_lot_of_numbers/339149.html [accessed 20.07.11].

7. http://thinkexist.com/quotation/setting_a_goal_is_not_the_main_thing-it_is/151192.html [accessed 20.07.11].

8. http://www.quotelady.com/subjects/plan.html [accessed 20.07.11].

Chapter 6

1. http://www.quotationspage.com/quote/1171.html [accessed 20.07.11].
2. http://quotationsbook.com/quote/383/ [accessed 20.07.11].
3. http://www.1-famous-quotes.com/quote/728889 [accessed 20.07.11].
4. http://www.imdb.com/title/tt0314062/quotes [accessed 20.07.11].

Chapter 7

1. http://www.searchquotes.com/quotation/You_are_always_a_student,_never_a_master._You_have_to_keep_moving_forward./109292/ [accessed 20.07.11].
2. http://www.searchquotes.com/quotation/The_first_assistant_director_is_just_so_important_that_the_choice_of_that_person_is_critical_to_the_/68649/ [accessed 20.07.11].
3. http://www.searchquotes.com/quotation/Executive_ability_is_deciding_quickly_and_getting_somebody_else_to_do_the_work./11887/ [accessed 20.07.11].
4. http://www.searchquotes.com/quotation/Any_time_you_talk_about_the_look_of_the_film,_it's_not_just_the_director_and_the_director_of_photogr/166186/ [accessed 20.07.11].
5. http://thinkexist.com/quotation/beware_of_the_person_who_can-t_be_bothered_by/331975.html [accessed 20.07.11].
6. http://thinkexist.com/quotation/advertising_is_totally_unnecessary-unless_you/209986.html [accessed 20.07.11].
7. http://www.brainyquote.com/quotes/authors/m/michelangelo.html [accessed 20.07.11].

Chapter 8

1. http://thinkexist.com/quotation/hire_people_who_are_better_than_you_are-then/203773.html [accessed 20.07.11].
2. http://www.searchquotes.com/quotation/Make_the_hard_ones_look_easy_and_the_easy_ones_look_hard./97457/ [accessed 20.07.11].
3. http://www.imdb.com/name/nm0000399/bio [accessed 20.07.11].
4. http://quotationsbook.com/quote/10418/ [accessed 20.07.11].
5. http://www.brainyquote.com/quotes/keywords/accident.html [accessed 20.07.11].
6. http://thinkexist.com/quotation/the_secret_of_all_victory_lies_in_the/215718.html [accessed 20.07.11].
7. Schlitz D. The gambler. Sung by Kenny Rogers; 1978.
8. http://www.searchquotes.com/quotation/A_good_director's_not_sure_when_he_gets_on_the_set_what_he's_going_to_do./88813/ [accessed 20.07.11].
9. http://thinkexist.com/quotation/never_put_off_till_tomorrow_what_you_can_do_today/146619.html [accessed 20.07.11].

References

Chapter 9

1. http://thinkexist.com/quotation/film-editing-is-now-something-almost-everyone-can/395422.html [accessed 20.07.11].
2. http://www.brainyquote.com/quotes/quotes/r/richarddon337513.html [accessed 20.07.11].
3. http://thinkexist.com/quotation/if_you_do_not_change_direction-you_may_end_up/214079.html [accessed 20.07.11].
4. http://thinkexist.com/quotation/nothing_will_work_unless_you_do/215802.html [accessed 20.07.11].
5. http://www.searchquotes.com/quotation/For_I_am_not_so_enamoured_of_my_own_opinions_that_I_disregard_what_others_may_think_of_them./99188/ [accessed 20.07.11].
6. http://www.imdb.com/title/tt0072431/trivia?tr=tr0733512 [accessed 20.07.11].

Chapter 10

1. http://www.brainyquote.com/quotes/quotes/r/redadair195665.html [accessed 20.07.11].
2. http://www.brainyquote.com/quotes/quotes/j/johnlennon167341.html [accessed 20.07.11].
3. http://thinkexist.com/quotation/music_is_the_shorthand_of_emotion/144779.html [accessed 20.07.11].
4. http://people.virginia.edu/~rlk3p/desource/quotes.html [accessed 20.07.11].
5. http://www.dictionary-quotes.com/things-should-be-made-as-simple-as-possible-but-not-any-simpler-albert-einstein/ [accessed 20.07.11].

Chapter 11

1. http://thinkexist.com/quotation/my_play_was_a_complete_success-the_audience_was_a/7438.html [accessed 20.07.11].
2. http://www.imdb.com/name/nm0000233/bio [accessed 20.07.11].
3. http://www.brainyquote.com/quotes/authors/w/w_clement_stone.html [accessed 22.07.11].
4. http://www.searchquotes.com/quotation/If_you_would_know_the_value_of_money,_go_and_try_to_borrow_some./19230/ [accessed 22.07.11].
5. http://www.quotegarden.com/guillemets-quotes.html [accessed 22.07.11].
6. http://thinkexist.com/quotation/when_i_let_go_of_what_i_am-i_become_what_i_might/340907.html [accessed 22.07.11].

Index

Page numbers in *italics* indicate boxes and figures.

Index

Index

Financing, of films (*Cont.*)
family members, 17
"gap financing" ("bridge loans"), 43
key points, *18, 43*
"negative pick-up" deal, 42–43
options, 17
and proximity to power, 18
star value, importance of, 23, *24*
using credit cards, 40–41
using pre-sales, 41–42
see also Budgeting
First impression, making a, 160–161, *161*
Fuqua, Antoine, 33

G

Gaffer, 78, 83
"Gap financing" ("bridge loans"), 43
Gatekeepers, 24, *24*, 30
Gibson, Mel, 17, 41
Goldblum, Jeff, 182
Good acting, 53
Grips and/or electrics (G&E department), 108–109, *109*

H

Haneke, Michael, 54
Hanks, Tom, 171
Hip pocketing, 192
Hitchcock, Alfred, 51
"Hold" days, 79
Holding, *59*
Horace, 8
Horror movies, 166
Hurt Locker, The, 166

I

IMDBPro.com, 29
"In the can," *25*
Independent film financing, 17

Inserts, 143
International pre-sales, 41
Internet Movie Data-base (IMDB), *12*

J

Jackson, Peter, 39, 196
Jaws, 9, 176
Josie and the Pussycats, 76
Jurassic Park, 182
Juxtaposition of images, 158, *158*

K

Keitel, Harvey, 24
King Kong, 166
Kubrick, Stanley, 3

L

Last looks, 146
Lawyers, involvement in movie making, 47–48, *48*
"Letter of intent (LOI)," 33–34
Limitations, relation with creativity, 8–9
Location scheduling, 65–66
interior *versus* exterior locations, 66
shoot-out, 66
see also Scheduling, for shooting out of order
Location scouts, 58–59
Locked script, 71, *71*
Lock-ups, *113*
Looping, session, 170–171, *172*
Lord of the Rings, The, 41, 196
Lord of the Rings: The Return of the King, 166
Lost in Translation, 39
"Low budget" filmmaking, 76–77, *76*
Lumet, Sidney, 69

M

Made for Each Other, 162
Marketing and distribution, of movie, 186–187
getting a distributor, 194–195, *195*

206

Index